# BEING V↑SUAL

## Raising a Generation of Innovative Thinkers

**BETTE FETTER**

GRAPE LOT
PRESS

Published by Grape Lot Press
PO Box 5504, Elgin, IL 60121

Library of Congress Control Number: 2012944283

Printed by Hagg Press, Inc., Elgin, Illinois

Cover and Interior Design: Katie Hofer
Illustrations: Bill Duca

Printed in the United States of America

ISBN 978-0-9822094-9-3

"At a time when we are testing our kids to oblivion, how refreshing to hear that it may not be the answer. As a writer and a mother of four, I'm not at all surprised by Bette Fetter's claim that most kids need visual stimulation to learn. In *Being Visual* she shares her life-long passion for teaching and the arts — and shows how they come together to create tomorrow's innovators."

— **Lee Woodruff**, *New York Times* bestselling co-author of *In an Instant* and "CBS This Morning" contributor

"Over the past 25 years as an educator, I have specialized in working with kids who carry the label of either having ADD, dyslexia, Asperger's or autism. I have observed a vast increase in the number of these students, and *Being Visual* brings fresh light into an arena where far too many people have become lost. The future will undoubtedly bring more visual learners; the disconnect between the education system and these learners will become a vast chasm if we continue on our present course. *Being Visual* is a strong step in the right direction, and should be required reading for anyone involved in education, parenting or the arts in today's visual generation."

— **Jeffrey Freed**, co-author of *Right-Brain Children in a Left-Brained World: Unlocking the Potential of Your ADD Child*

"*Being Visual: Raising a Generation of Innovative Thinkers*, by Bette Fetter, is a welcome addition to the books on understanding and reaching visual-spatial learners — those with strong right-hemispheric gifts. Embroidered with delightful visual representations of the ideas, the book weaves theory, personal experience and helpful suggestions into a unique tapestry. This is a powerful call to reinstate the arts in education. There are instructive sections on quiet, Montessori-based education, autism, Alzheimer's, and art. Recommended for parents, teachers and all caring readers."

— **Linda K. Silverman**, Ph.D., Director, Gifted Development Center, author of *Upside-Down Brilliance: The Visual-Spatial Learner*

*I dedicate this book to:*

*God*

*Bill*
*Laurie, Emily, Liz and Matt*

*Artists and Educators*

# 4

## SEE, TOUCH, DO LEARNING

# 5

## SPECIAL OPPORTUNITIES

# 6

## TEACHING "HOW TO"

## THANK YOU

I dedicate this book first and foremost to God, my steady and faithful companion. He set me on a life path, long before I realized how intentional it had all been. God birthed me with a love of art, passion for children and spirit of curiosity and determination. He then set me on a path of what I thought were circumstances and life choices, but were, in fact, His thoughtful design. I am thankful for the divine assignments and appointments, people and places God put in my path to educate, equip, love and help me, in ways too numerous to name here, and for His wisdom, guidance, trust and faithfulness. It takes a village to raise a child and the village He provided me has led to a rich life, wonderful family and friends, joyful work and the birth of this book.

I would like to thank Bill, my dear and generous husband. I am thankful for all the ways he has encouraged, loved and believed all these years. He always saw the big picture, the possibilities of how far Young Rembrandts could reach. I appreciate Bill for expanding my vision, being my wise and steady counsel and for the time spent doing this work together.

I am thankful to Laurie, Emmy, Liz and Matt for being my children, my students and now my most treasured friends. They gave my life purpose and have been a constant source of delight, discovery, love and joy. I so enjoyed the time they spent discovering themselves through the arts and am eternally grateful we are doing this life together.

I would like to thank artists, dancers, musicians, actors, writers, directors and moviemakers everywhere. They bring to life what the mind can imagine and the heart delights in; they open our eyes to better see the world as it is and give breath and life to what it can be. We are blessed that they share themselves, their passion and their vision with us all.

I thank the leaders and families of Children's Theatre of Elgin. Together we spent thousands of hours, worked on dozens of performances and blessed hundreds and hundreds of children and adults alike. My time with this group enabled me to grow as an individual and experience first-hand the power of theater, dance and music to transform and impact young lives. I thank them for their heart, passion for the arts and for giving so much of themselves to our youth.

A special thanks to educators, for their passion to affect change by teaching and training in what have become increasingly challenging circumstances. On behalf of countless children and parents everywhere, I thank them for seeing the limitless potential and all they do to enrich the hearts and minds of those they teach.

Thanks to Christine Doornbos, who poked and prodded me to teach her children how to draw. Thanks to Deborah LaPorte for bringing Montessori into my heart and home. Thanks to Jeanine Halverson for recognizing the uniqueness of the work my early students were doing and encouraging me to take it to a larger audience.

I would like to thank the Young Rembrandts community. It has been and continues to be a lovely journey. We have a very special village of passionate teachers, trainers, and businessmen and women who have dedicated themselves to bringing more art to their local communities. The members of our Home Office team have been many over the years. Each and everyone has contributed in his or her unique way. Their passion, integrity, creativity and commitment to excellence are inspiring.

Many thanks to the people who have encouraged, organized, and contributed stories to this book. I would like to thank Barb Goeske for sharing her heart, wisdom, experience and resources for special needs students. Thanks to Bill Duca, Erika Hintz, Katie Hofer and Monique Wallen for illustrating, editing, organizing, designing and being in the visual conversation with me. A special thanks to Mimi Lytle, a dear friend who's been a divine appointment on several occasions in my life. Each time she read and edited this manuscript, she encouraged and challenged me to make it better. Her kindness, wisdom, guidance and help birthing this book have been a tremendous blessing.

Everyone is a genius. But if you judge a fish by its ability to climb a tree, it will live its whole life believing it's stupid.

- Albert Einstein

# INTRODUCTION

A shift has happened. Times have changed and the world is flat. As part of a global supply chain, we have to run faster to keep up. We need to "up our game" to compete. Businesses need ideas, strategies and competencies that deliver a competitive advantage. The current business climate requires creativity, innovation and strategists at every level of enterprise. Technology, global access and competitiveness require that we know how to think, what questions to ask, which ideas to pursue.

Educators are preparing the workforce of tomorrow. Unfortunately, we have an outdated education system, and it's getting worse. In a failing effort to improve outcomes, legislators have increased testing. Their focus is on better test results, not better teaching. Schools are producing test takers, while businesses need thinkers and innovators. There's a disconnect, and it is catching up to us.

There is scientific evidence that the left and right hemispheres of our brains have unique qualities that directly affect the way we think, experience and perceive the world. Our dominant hemisphere also affects the way we learn, what careers we choose, if we'll know what kind of questions to ask and which ideas to pursue. Currently, our education system is focused on developing linear, logical, language-oriented thought processes, a very left-brain bias that works for 25% of the student population. These students learn sequentially, are detail-oriented and thrive in the world of words and data. However, while these are valuable skills, they're not enough for tomorrow.

Fortunately, there's a tremendous, game-changing resource, present in classrooms all across the globe. Right now. Everywhere. Its been overlooked, misunderstood and undervalued for far too long. It's the quality businesses will pay for, the key ingredient of the Conceptual Age, the ingredient we need to enhance and move beyond logical, linear thought processes. This resource lies in the right side of our mind. It's the place ideas live. It's the home of creativity, innovation and divergent thinking.

The right side of our brain is home to visual-spatial thinking. Students who are right-brain dominant are big picture, pattern seeking and holistic thinkers, seeing the "whole" before they see the "how". They're visual, conceptual, creative and our future innovators. These thinkers also possess strong spatial skills, key to high-level patterning and math skills. But they're also the fish stuck in trees, struggling in our current education system. Visual-spatial thinkers thrive in the world of images, not words. They need to *see,* to think. When they don't see, they can't think. When they don't think, they don't learn.

While our fish have been stuck in trees, the water they need is being eliminated. The arts, critical to developing visual-spatial thinking, have been cut, or at best relegated to non-essential, part-time status. And yet, these subjects cultivate conceptual thinking, innovation and collaboration in ways that academic subject matter cannot. The arts are too often considered non-career subjects, valuable for hobbies, and much less important than science, technology, engineering and math (STEM). But just as creativity is not limited to the arts, right-brain thinking is not limited to the arts. Many of our science, technology, engineering and math students are visual-spatial learners. There are brilliant minds not being developed properly, and even worse, feeling inept, because their gifts are not understood.

How do we get our fish out of trees and empowered to perform in order to change the trajectory of our nation? We refill the pool, get them back in the water and let them swim. We adapt teaching strategies to better reach our visual-spatial learners. We speak in a language our visual-spatial learners understand, encouraging and empowering them to fully use their gifts. Visual arts are an essential component because they provide the training and tools to see, think, imagine and communicate. And while this will be enormously beneficial for our visual students, there is a right side to all of us.

# Right & Left-Brain Remodeling

I am an artistic, creative right-brain visual thinker with strong language and analytical skills. I have heard this is an unusual combination. My husband, Eric, is a left-brain, linear thinker and successful project manager. Recently, I approached my hubby about remodeling the living room. I wanted to remove a wall, open up the entryway and make some changes to the downstairs color scheme. I described my vision in great detail, sharing design ideas, aesthetic details, and color choices, but he didn't "see" what I saw.

After several attempts to convey my vision and its benefits, I realized I needed to change my approach and translate my vision into language Eric would be more comfortable with. So I carefully outlined a work plan and used data to show how the remodel would increase our home value, provide more living space and increase the flow and efficiency. I had thought about these kinds of things when first picturing the project, but hadn't included them when I was talking to him.

Eventually, Eric agreed to the remodeling project. He never envisioned the project the same way I did, but now he had facts, figures and projections that allowed him to see it in a way that made sense to him. While we do "get" how each other thinks, it was our overall trust in each other and experience in similar situations that enabled us to move forward. In the end, the remodel was a great success, and we were both delighted with the results. With the wall removed, the new trim installed and walls painted, Eric is now able to physically see the vision I had for the room.

- Monique Wallen
*Marketing Professional & Graphic Designer*

# 1

# Getting to Know
# the Right

> " In a world of drastic change, it is the learners who inherit the future. The learned usually find themselves equipped to live in a world that no longer exists. "
>
> - Eric Hoffer[1]

**I AM A VISUAL PERSON. I SEE IN PICTURES.** I think in pictures. I process, communicate and learn in pictures and images. I am a visual learner. When I hear information, my mind converts the data into pictures for understanding, remembering and storing for future reference. When I explain concepts or share my thoughts, I first see the thoughts, then convert them into language others can understand. When information is presented to me accompanied by images, there is less translation needed, so I understand and process the information more quickly. Being visual is not unique. It's estimated that 75% of people rely on their visual skills to learn.

I am also artistic. As a child, I was given paint, pastels, paper and a steady stream of art and craft supplies. I love art. I love to do art, see art and make art. My brother affectionately calls me an "art nerd." I am emotionally moved by visual experiences. I am attracted to the beauty of line, pattern and color. As an artistic and visual person, the world appears to me as a series of patterns, spaces, shapes and colors. After all these years, I am still excited by a new set of colored pencils — so many colors and so much possibility.

I am also a teacher. My fine arts degree and exposure to Montessori education enabled me to develop a unique approach to teaching art and drawing, an approach that combined the demonstration and step-by-step instruction I longed for as a child. I realized later that drawing, the fundamental skill of visual art, was a critical component of my success as a visual learner. The ability to visualize to learn, draw to remember, and create visuals to communicate empowered me.

> " *...visualize to learn, draw to remember, and create visuals to communicate...* "

I am also a businesswoman, an entrepreneur, a leader, a visionary. This was a big surprise to me. Some people told me a fine arts degree would make me virtually unemployable. I didn't understand the risk, but knew I had to do art. Much later in life, I realized that many of my strengths in business — being visual, relational, collaborative, innovative — had been developed through my participation in the arts. Visual art, theatre and music had all contributed to the development of my discrimination and patterning skills, divergent thinking and the ability to consider multiple solutions to a problem.

Through my years of business, education and study, I have observed some key differences in how people experience and perceive the world. They also affect our ability to learn, our career choices and our working styles. These differences of perception have created two types of thinkers which coincide with the two hemispheres of the brain: right-brain contextual, big picture, conceptual thinkers; and left-brain logical, focused, piece-by-piece, step-by-step thinkers.

While it has been clearly documented that both sides of the brain are involved in almost all mental processes, each hemisphere does have specialized expertise. The nuances of left and right-brain functions profoundly affect the way we process information and experience the world. In his book, *The Master and His Emissary*, psychiatrist and author Iain McGilchrist shares, "...each hemisphere attends to the world in a different way — and the ways are consistent. The right hemisphere underwrites breadth and flexibility of attention, where the left hemisphere brings to bear focused attention. This has the related consequence that the right hemisphere sees things whole, and in context, where the left hemisphere sees things abstracted from context, and broken into parts, from which it constructs a 'whole': something quite different."[2]

Our education system has long been focused on the details abstracted from context, developing left-brain thinking. This has led to an imbalance, with our right side being undervalued and undernourished. But today's world needs the expertise of our right hemisphere. By understanding what the right side of our brain has to offer and how it best functions, we can adjust and improve educational strategies for a smarter tomorrow.

## Our Time Has Come

Children born in 2011 will enter the work force by 2035. We can only imagine what that will look like or what jobs will be available for them. We must reconsider how to prepare them for the future. Life will not present itself as A, B, C or D questions and answers. Our kids will need to know *how to think*. They will have to ask questions — the right questions — to access the vast amount of information so readily available. They will have to discern what information is relevant and decide what to do with that information. They will need to know how to work independently and in teams, to communicate effectively, understand the needs of others, seek truth and generate original thoughts and ideas in an increasingly complex world. These are visual-spatial, right-brain kinds of abilities. Our schools know how to teach to the analytical left side of our brains. Now we need to be more intentional about reaching and developing the right side, *the visual in all of us*.

There is a profound shift at hand. Leaders from all walks of life are calling for change, because they see the world changing around them. We are no longer living and competing in our separate corners of the world. The world is flat, and we're all in this together. In his book, *A Whole New Mind*, author Daniel Pink talks about our changing world and what it will take to succeed in the uncertain future. According to Pink, abundance, automation and Asia have created a shift of global proportions, moving us from the Information Age into the Conceptual Age. With information, technology and global access at our fingertips, we have to decide what we are going to do with such power and possibility. What's next? What should we make? What should we do? How do we connect it, use it, and adapt it to make the world a better place, to advance humankind? This is the domain of right-brain thinking. Our time has come.

Pink writes, "Today, the defining skills of the previous era — the 'left-brain' capabilities that powered the Information Age — are necessary but no longer sufficient. And the capabilities we once disdained or thought frivolous — the 'right-brain' qualities of inventiveness, empathy, joyfulness and meaning — increasingly will determine who flourishes and who flounders. For individuals, families, and organizations, professional success and personal fulfillment now require a whole new mind."[3]

```
analytical
   logical
    linear
sequential
  detailed
```

## Analytical, Rational, Logical Left

Those who are left-brain dominant are very logical. They approach the world in a rational, methodical, one right answer kind of way. Management expert and writer Peter Drucker describes these thinkers as having the "ability to acquire and apply theoretical and analytical knowledge."[4] Left-brain thinking is also known as auditory-sequential thinking. Auditory-sequential people think in a step-by-step, linear manner, understanding separate parts before they understand the whole. They have a good sense of time and think most efficiently when material is presented audibly.

Since words are processed serially, people who are auditory-sequential tend to have strong language skills. They think in words. This, combined with excellent short-term memory, makes them good at spelling and vocabulary. Strong auditory skills make them adept at following oral directions and listening to lectures. They're often strong writers which, when combined with their sequencing skills, enable them to create well-organized paragraphs and essays — skills that align well with traditional teaching methods.

Because auditory-sequential thinkers (left-brain) are logical and think in a progression of steps, they learn information one step at a time, in a linear fashion. They learn best through drill and repetition, building skill and gaining mastery, as they approach more complex subject matter. They think through problems very logically, are comfortable with multiple choice and true false tests, and are content knowing there is one right answer to a question. Learning sequentially, organizing thoughts, making lists, taking tests and thinking through problems logically are more skills that align well with traditional teaching methods.

Auditory-sequential thinkers are convergent thinkers. Convergent thinking is analytical, deductive thinking where ideas are examined for logical validity. Very Spock-like. Arithmetic, with one right answer to a problem, is representative of convergent thinking. Their minds contain neatly organized, relevant data. When questioned, they query the well-organized data for the appropriate, logical answer. Standardized testing works well for these students.

## Intuitive, Holistic, Big Picture Right

In sharp contrast to left-brain linear thinking, right-brain thinking is non-linear, holistic, intuitive, relational and instinctive. Those who are right-brain dominant are visual rather than verbal and have a keen awareness of size, space and relationships, hence the term "visual-spatial". Right-brain, visual-spatial thinkers are multi-dimensional, conceptual, big picture thinkers that see the whole before the separate, smaller parts.

intuitive
**BIG** PICTURE
NoN-LiNeAr
RELATIONAL
HOLISTIC

The right side of our mind gives meaning to what the left can analyze. While the left orders and reasons sequentially, the right side is able to synthesize, see many things at once and consider them as a whole. Researcher and scientist Roger W. Sperry wrote, "The right hemisphere reasoned holistically, recognized patterns, and interpreted emotions and non-verbal expressions."[5] So while the left is managing the details, the right is seeing the big picture. Right-brain dominant people innovate, interpret, and bring meaning to the text and logic of our left-brain.

The right side of our brain is also home to divergent thinking, the root of innovation. Divergent thinking follows many lines of thought, usually arriving at new and original solutions to problems. Because visual-spatials are non-linear and holistic, this type of thinking is very natural for them. They have loads of relevant data in their mental libraries, but instead of accessing it one subject at a time, they tend to view it simultaneously, the perfect set up for divergent thought processes.

## Out of the Box

Divergent thinking is out-of-the-box thinking, usually associated with creativity. While left-brain, convergent thinking is great for deductive, analytical needs, divergent thinking is critical for creative problem solving and idea generation. Schools train and measure convergent thinking abilities, but science, technology, business, innovation and life are desperate for divergent thinking.

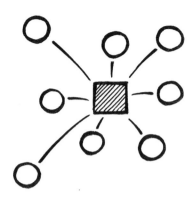

Right-brain, visual-spatial thinking requires visualizing. No visualizing, no thinking. No thinking, no learning. These people live in the world of images, seeing, processing, and translating everything into pictures in order to learn and remember. Because of their strong spatial skills, they tend to see the world three-dimensionally, enabling them to perform complex mental tasks and processes, sometimes easier than simple ones. Visual-spatial reasoning has the potential for true genius — the place of invention, scientific breakthroughs and world changing innovation.

Yet our visual-spatials often struggle in school. The images and tools they need to learn are often missing in language heavy, linear, logical school systems. Because they learn holistically and conceptually, they have a difficult time with sequential learning, memorization and timed testing. Linda Silverman, researcher, author and Director of the Gifted Development Center, writes, "Visual-spatial learners often struggle in the areas in which auditory-sequential learners succeed. These children understand space better than time, and often lose track of time. They are holistic, rather than detail-oriented. They focus on ideas and may miss formatting requirements, such as punctuation, capitalization, spelling, grammar, and syntax. It is easy for them to recognize patterns. They may be excellent at mathematical reasoning, but make careless mistakes in calculation. They are divergent thinkers rather than convergent thinkers, often generating unusual solutions to problems."[6]

Left-brain and right-brain thinkers approach the world very differently. One is thinking logically, loves details and manages time well. The other is big picture, non-linear, not logical and sees the whole before the parts. There is a huge gap here. The problem is that society and our education system favors one of these thinkers. But we need what our right has to offer and its time we make some serious changes.

## Multiple Solutions

Making connections between disparate things is a critical component to true creativity. Innovation — the process of finding and applying new ideas — is right-brain divergent thinking, a wonderful attribute of the visual-spatial mind. Elliot Eisner, professor of Art and Education at Stanford University, has long researched  and spoken on the value of art education. In his book, *The Arts and the Creation of Mind*, he credits art as the subject that helps children see "there are multiple solutions to a problem" and make "good judgments about qualitative relationships."[7] While the arts do serve this purpose well, they're not solely a function of the arts.

Multiple solutions and innovative ways to view and analyze a subject is the domain of the visual-spatial mind. Artists, poets and musicians tend to be visual-spatials, but it's not limited to the arts. Many scientists, mathematicians, engineers and computer programmers are visual-spatial thinkers. We may not think of scientists as right-brained or as visuals, yet many well-known scientists and innovators have been able to "see" the inventions that reshaped our world.

Da Vinci, Edison and Einstein, all brilliant scientists and innovators, had difficulty in school, especially with reading, writing and computation skills. Albert Einstein, considered one of the most prolific intellects in history, thought in a stream of pictures. It's documented that a critical component of his theory of relativity came after he "saw" himself riding a wave of light. Einstein was intentional about using his visual-spatial skills, filling his thoughts with data and peer discussion, then setting his thoughts aside to pursue some non-related pleasurable activity. As he sailed or played his violin, his mind sorted, considered, connected and imagined, later bringing forth insightful steams of pictures that led to scientific and technological innovations.

The creative genius Leonardo da Vinci saw everything as connected. Da Vinci used the connective properties of his innovative mind as a scientist, engineer, artist, inventor and philosopher. His ability to draw was a powerful thinking aid. Drawing allowed him to illustrate what he observed and imagined. His ability to draw allowed him to create visual images — incredibly detailed pictures — of his inventions. Words cannot do justice to the incredible images Leonardo left behind. These drawings allowed him to record his own thoughts, but also allowed him to share what he could see so vividly in his mind's eye.

The notebooks of Neils Bohr, one of the most influential scientists of the 20th century, were filled with pictures and words, absent of mathematical and scientific equations. The ability to illustrate a complex concept was a key component in the discovery of DNA. Several scientists were working simultaneously to uncover the complex nature of DNA. At Cambridge University, James Watson and Francis Crick made physical models of DNA to narrow down the possibilities. Eventually, they were successful in building the three-dimensional model that demonstrated its complicated physical structure. This physical, spatial model enabled them to finalize key elements of their hypothesis and led to a shared Nobel Prize in 1962. Now, when students learn about DNA in school, illustrations of the three-dimensional model facilitate understanding much more than the volumes and volumes of words it would take to explain it.

In her book, *Thinking in Pictures*, scientist and engineer Temple Grandin shares, "I think in pictures. Words are like a second language to me. I translate both spoken and written language into full-color movies, complete with sound, which run like a VCR tape in my head." Temple, a person with high-functioning autism, is also an author and inventor. With a bachelor's degree in psychology and a master's and doctoral degree in animal science, she considers her ability to see in pictures a tremendous advantage as an equipment designer in the livestock industry. "Every design problem I ever solved started with my ability to visualize and see the world in pictures."[8]

## Biased Education Systems

Our education system favors the auditory-sequential thinker. We teach, test, measure and value their skills above those of the visual-spatial thinker. This crisis is affecting the majority of our student population. According to Linda Silverman's book, *Upside-Down Brilliance: The Visual-Spatial Learner*, it is currently estimated that 30% of the population are primarily visual-spatial dominant.

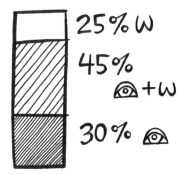

Visual-spatial thinking, in conjunction with thinking in words, is estimated at 45% of the population, while the other 25% use words as their primary thinking mode. That means 75% of students use their dominant visual skills to think. The other 25% still use visual skills, but to a lesser degree.[9]

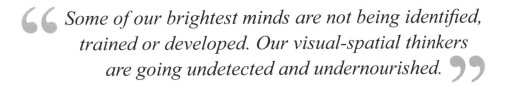

> *Some of our brightest minds are not being identified, trained or developed. Our visual-spatial thinkers are going undetected and undernourished.*

Our linear, sequential, language heavy, test-crazed education systems effectively serve 25% of our student population. The other 75% include our future scientists, technology specialists, engineers, mathematicians, computer specialists and innovators, along with our artists, poets and musicians. These kids don't understand how they're different, but they can feel it. Not only do they suffer while trying to fit into language-intensive classrooms, their innate gifts are not being addressed, and they are often unaware of their value and strengths. Some of our brightest minds are not being identified, trained or developed. Our visual-spatial thinkers are going undetected and undernourished.

**1**

## Creativity in Science, Technology, Engineering & Math (STEM)

In an effort to improve educational outcomes in science and math, the federal government recently announced plans to promote and fund learning opportunities in science, technology, engineering and math (STEM). Business and non-profit foundations have been invited to join in the efforts and are responding with initiatives to help fund learning programs.

This "Educate to Innovate" program also recognizes the impact teachers have in making learning successful. "The quality of math and science teachers is the most important single factor influencing whether students will succeed or fail in science, technology, engineering and math," President Obama said. "Passionate educators with issue expertise can make all the difference, enabling hands-on learning that truly engages students — including girls and underrepresented minorities — and preparing them to tackle the grand challenges of the 21st century such as increasing energy independence, improving people's health, protecting the environment, and strengthening national security."[10]

However, educators with subject matter expertise are not enough to make learning successful. Our educators have to understand how to better teach visual-spatial students. As wonderful as the education and funding opportunities are, we risk wasting these opportunities if we don't make adjustments to the way we're teaching these subjects. *In the Mind's Eye*, by Thomas G. West, finds that "Visual and spatial modes of thought seem well suited to dealing with certain complex problems and are often closely associated with major creative achievements in the sciences as well as the arts. Visual-spatial abilities can play a much more important role in major creative accomplishments; in many different fields, even when they are not commonly thought to be highly visual; than is commonly recognized."[11] The word-oriented world is changing and our computer based, technology driven, visually-oriented world requires a new kind of training. What are we doing to develop visual-spatial thinking? Are we being intentional about developing minds like Einstein, Edison or da Vinci? Or hoping they survive education to still invent and contribute?

The challenges of teaching visual-spatial students reach far beyond the elementary classroom. Middle schools, high schools and colleges need to address their visual learners. There are enormous numbers of these students, underachieving at alarming rates and they don't know why. But the difficulty has never been with the child. It lies in the inability of our schools to speak to them in a language they can understand.

## Verbal & Visual Literacy

For many years, literacy has been defined as the ability to read and write text, but scientific evidence is changing the way people think about literacy. Recognizing we are a world of diverse individuals with a wide range and type of literacies, including visuals, UNESCO, The United Nations Educational, Scientific and Cultural Organization, has redefined literacy. According to UNESCO, "Literacy is the ability to identify, understand, interpret, create, communicate, compute and use printed and written materials associated with varying contexts. Literacy involves a continuum of learning in enabling individuals to achieve their goals, to develop their knowledge and potential, and to participate fully in their community and wider society." This definition suggests literacy includes all forms of written and printed communication, which embraces visual imagery and visual communications. It also reminds us that when individuals use their full range of abilities, they develop their knowledge and potential, enabling them to participate wholly in society.

> *Literacy is the ability to identify, understand, interpret, create, communicate, compute and use printed and written materials associated with varying contexts.*
>
> - UNESCO

*Visual literacy*, the ability to read, write and respond to and interpret visual images, has become critical in today's world where images have become an essential part of communication, and, "the use of literacy must also change and adapt — for example, when bookkeepers have to handle complex computer [programs] rather than recording figures in a ledger, their literacy needs change. As society increasingly creates wealth by gathering information and processing it into useful knowledge, literacy demands also change."[12]

It's no longer sufficient to focus singularly on the written word. Visual literacy is not reserved for the right-brain visual-spatials; it's a skill that's critical for both left and right-brain individuals. As educators and parents, we must broaden our approach and be intentional about developing both visual and verbal skills in all learners.

>
> *...learning to see and create visual images must also be recognized as essential to the learning process.*

## Developing Visual Literacy

*Seeing* is essential to the right-brain thinking process, so *learning to see* and *create* visual images must also be recognized as essential to the learning process. The world has always been  visual and it's increasing exponentially, with television, technology and computers. Yet text-heavy, linear educational environments are often lacking in appropriate or engaging imagery. There are words, words, words — lectures, lectures, lectures — but not enough visuals. Remember, the majority of students and adults prefer to use visual-spatial processing skills because they are much faster, richer, more multidimensional and comprehensive. So along with respecting visual-spatial thinking needs, we must find ways to increase use of visuals so we can *see to learn*. Teaching that includes visuals will benefit both left and right-brain learners.

In *Developing Visual Literacy in Science K - 8*, authors Comer, Troutman and Vasquez remind us that every brain relies on the eyes as the primary channel of sensory input. "Remarkable, unbelievably, the brain is capable of absorbing 36,000 visual images, every hour. How can this imponderable ability be true? It is because the sophisticated visual capacity of our brain system is beyond the conscious processing of our mind. Research approximates that between 70% to 90% of the information received by the brain is through visual channels. Though our auditory and kinesthetic modes of 'sensing' are complex, the brain's dominant and most efficient sensory filter for most information is our eyes."[13]

> " *...the brain is capable of absorbing 36,000 visual images, every hour.* "

There are tremendous, almost limitless opportunities to use the remarkable capabilities of the eyes by including a broader range of visuals when we teach. In order to process oral and written language, our visual-spatials spend a lot of time and energy translating language into mental pictures. It's a tiresome, even discouraging process, causing them to miss significant information and details. Rather than relying on words, words and more words, we can reduce the time spent translating and provide more information visually. Researchers have shown that "adding visuals to verbal (text and or auditory) learning can result in significant gains in basic and higher-order learning."[14] Illustrations, visual aids and hands-on models enable visual students to learn much more effectively then a reliance solely on the printed word.

As we become more adept at incorporating visuals for reading or teaching, we have to be sure the images we use make sense. It's essential that we use images as skillfully as we use words, carefully considering them to be sure they tell the whole story, logically and with the necessary amount of detail. When images are unclear, or don't convey the subject matter well, it leads to confusion, discouragement and misunderstanding.

## Critical Visual Skills

There are also significant abilities gained when children develop *critical* visual skills, because "the ability to view text and images critically and purposefully is an analytical process that increases learners' social, environmental, spiritual, political and critical consciousness."[15] Just as we learn to read and consider the content of what we are reading, so we need to know how to see, understand and evaluate the content of the visual image or experience. According to researchers Falihi and Wason-Ellam, critical visual literacy "allows the viewer to engage in the experience of gathering information and ideas contained in an image and place them in context."[16] Learners and observers need to discern value, meaning and have the ability to use and create visuals in meaningful ways.

Researchers Duffelmeyer and Ellerston have concluded that critically literate people need to know the world of text is not literal but constructed, they need to be able to develop and demonstrate awareness as a composer and reader of text, and develop the ability as a communicator and reader.[17] This challenges us to reconsider the way we view the visual arts in relation to literacy. It's no longer sufficient to use a few images and assume kids will know what they mean. Critical visual literacy must include the development of observation and discernment skills for students to read visual text. They also need to know how to compose their own visuals as communication tools. The needs and goals of visual literacy are the same as verbal and written literacy and require the same systematic, codified methodology we use to teach reading and writing.

## Drawing is Visual Writing

Writing is the compositional element of reading. It's also a process of reflection and construction. As a literacy skill, writing is not optional. We expect everyone to be able to use written communication with some level of mastery. Drawing is the compositional form of being visual. Everyone needs to be able to write — *visually*. Drawing is visual writing. It's the fundamental form of written visual communication. *Visual literacy*, the ability to read, write and respond to and interpret visual images, "is not complete if critical visual writing, producing, composing are not experienced and practiced."[18]

## " *Drawing is visual writing.* "

Visual and verbal literacy requires us to be able to read and compose text. That means read and write words *and* read and write images. The ability to draw and communicate visually can no longer be seen as optional, or reserved for the small minority of children who have a natural inclination towards art. To be fully literate, our right-brain kids need to be able to read and write visually, but our left-brain, logical kids also live in a world of increasing visual interfaces. They, too, need to be fully literate, verbally and visually.

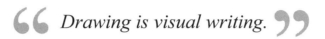

### Reading & Math are Visual

Training children to read and write visual symbols at a young age will increase their abilities in other areas of the classroom. Learning to evaluate and discern visually helps children develop patterning and differentiation skills, critical to all learning. Early success in reading requires the ability to recognize shapes and symbols, while being keenly aware of subtle differences. A child must be able to discern P from R, C from O, to read and apply meaning correctly. They also have to be able to write letters, with their subtle differences, and place them in order so others can read what they have to say.

In math, recognizing the difference between 6 and 9, 10 and 100 is quite significant, and the challenge increases with higher function applications. Math operations — addition, subtraction, multiplication and division — are communicated through the placement of numbers and the symbols used to represent the operation. Children have to know the value of the symbols, but also have the ability to discern shapes, relationships and placement as it relates to context. Visual understanding, differentiation, and sequencing are critical success factors. Training children to see patterns and distinguish visual differences will undergird their abilities in these key subjects.

$$2 + 5 = 7$$
$$2 \times 5 = 10$$
$$10 - 5 = 5$$
$$10 \div 5 = 2$$

## Art is Reading

Last year, there were several students consistently being pulled out of my art classroom. These kids were struggling with reading and needed some additional assistance. They spent the first half of art class in another room with reading specialists, rejoining us at the end of the lesson, which was media focused. I knew there was a benefit to them being in art class so I questioned the arrangement. Art and reading are both visual skills. Reading is about deciphering visual symbols. Art is about developing visual skills and learning to see and create symbols. I discussed the matter with the reading specialists and they gained a better understanding of the value of art class, especially in relation to the development of reading skills. The children have been in full attendance ever since.

-Kelly Field
*Elementary art teacher, Schaumburg, Illinois*

## Visual Vocabulary

Verbal literacy is significantly influenced by the depth and breadth of our vocabulary. Merriam-Webster's dictionary defines vocabulary as "a sum or stock of words employed by a language, group, individual, or work or in a field of knowledge."[19] The depth of our vocabulary directly affects our ability to communicate, comprehend reading material and our ability to acquire knowledge. Vocabulary is developed over time by listening, speaking, reading and instruction. Hearing, seeing and reading develops receptive, passive vocabulary. Productive, active vocabulary is acquired when we learn how to use words, place them in the right context and with the intended meaning.

Visual literacy also requires the development and mastery of vocabulary — a *visual vocabulary*. Visual literacy requires us to read, write and respond to and interpret visual images, and will require an understanding of visual images. A healthy visual vocabulary will also require the development of both passive and active language skills, but they will be passive and active *visual* vocabulary skills. So just as auditory-sequential learning intentionally develops oral and written vocabulary, our students need time and training to be intentional about developing their visual vocabulary skills.

> *Visual literacy also requires the development and mastery of vocabulary, a visual vocabulary.*

Pre-school children build their vocabulary by hearing and using words to speak. When they get to school, they are tasked with understanding the written word and connecting meaning to their oral vocabulary. Successful instruction includes strategies to help students decode new words and expand their literate vocabularies. Building a visual vocabulary will require many of the same techniques. Visual experience is quite natural, but the depth of that experience varies and is dependent on circumstance and culture.

Visual training that includes learning to see, draw and use visual images is critical to the development of a comprehensive visual vocabulary, the foundation of visual literacy. Once in school, like vocabulary, visual vocabulary development will require training to discern images and apply meaning. Visual vocabulary requires decoding skills and the ability to apply meaning from earlier visual experiences.

One of the most popular ways to help children expand their vocabularies is to read aloud to them. However, researchers suggest vocabulary growth was greater when teachers discussed meanings of words while reading. This applies to developing visual vocabulary. Even though we are adept at seeing, there's still a need to discuss and bring meaning to the visual images that accompany text.[20]

Like verbal vocabulary, the number of visual images children can create and use will be reflective of their visual vocabulary. The ability to use visuals to communicate requires the ability to create visual images. To do this, children need to know how to draw. Most kids communicate with a very limited visual vocabulary that includes drawings of rainbows, smiley faces and sunshine. To be more effective, they need to know how to draw a volume of familiar images, such as houses, cars, people, dogs, cats and so much more.

## Drawing Words

Learning to draw as an element of becoming literate has other distinct advantages that affect performance in other subject areas. When visual children are engaged in the act of drawing, there are tremendous opportunities to develop vocabulary. Drawing hamsters, dogs, bridges and farms gives children visuals for the nouns they're learning. Visual thinkers need to see to learn and require relevancy to remember, so teaching vocabulary while drawing provides them visual images of words. They see and draw the very picture memory they require in order to learn the word or concept.

Learning about and drawing a piece of "op art", full of concentric circles and intersecting lines, provides an unparalleled opportunity for vocabulary as well as memory and understanding. Horizontal, vertical and diagonal are important concepts, but learning those words while drawing horizontal, vertical and diagonal lines to place shapes or as part of a drawing gives children the multisensory reality of experience they need to make learning successful. Drawing shapes, understanding scale, proportions and relationships prepares kids with concepts later encountered in math, science and other subjects.

*Drawing shapes, understanding scale, proportions and relationships prepares kids with concepts later encountered in math, science and other subjects.*

## Making a Connection

When our son, Matt, was four years old, he attended an extended day pre-school program at a local Montessori school. I dropped him off at 9 am, and his Dad picked him up at 1 p.m. On Tuesdays, Matt stayed after school to attend a Young Rembrandts class, so his Dad picked him up at 1:45, just in time to be home when his sisters came home from school.

One particular warm spring day, I arrived home after teaching my own classes and was welcomed by the most delightfully colored sidewalks I had ever seen. We lived in a historic home on a large lot, in a beautiful neighborhood with sidewalks that edged the front yards. A long curved path connected the sidewalk and front door. As I approached our house, I saw that all of the expansive cement areas were filled with colored chalk drawings of birds and birdhouses. Pink, orange, blue and yellow birdhouses of every size adorned the walks with colorful birds flying around and between. It was obvious they had been drawn by the same young artist and looked very much like the birdhouse in a recent Young Rembrandts lesson.

As I entered the house through the kitchen door, I was met with more birdhouse drawings. There were papers and napkins strewn about the kitchen. Soon Matt came bounding in the room excitedly. He wanted to show me how to draw a birdhouse. It seemed he had already given his Dad and three sisters instruction, hence the bevy of birdhouse papers. We sat down and sure enough, step-by-step, Matt taught me how to draw birds and a birdhouse.

Matt had been in drawing class since he was three, and someone was always drawing at our house, so I was curious about his intense response this day. It was obvious something quite significant had happened in class, so after walking outside with Matt, viewing all of his work and hearing his birdhouse stories, I called his instructor. Without telling her why I was calling, I asked her to tell me about her class that day.

Miss Anne explained that while planning to teach the birdhouse lesson that day, she realized she had a birdhouse at home, still in its box. So she took the house, box and all to class with her. Once the kids were settled around the table, Anne pulled it out of the box much to the delight of her group. They talked about birds, what birds eat, where they live and why we use bird feeders and birdhouses. Before they started drawing, they talked about the shape of the house, its square base, triangle top and circular opening. Then they learned the shapes needed to draw the house and birds. The class proceeded as usual; everyone drew and colored their own birdhouse pictures.

Being able to see the actual birdhouse while drawing made a powerful impression on Matt that day. Young children already have a fondness for animals and birds, but seeing the birdhouse up close, hearing what it was and who would live in it, made a deeper connection. They saw it, touched it, talked about it, then drew and colored it, all while learning more about themselves and the birds around them.

## Auditory-Sequential vs Visual-Spatial Learners

Linda Silverman maps out the differences that auditory-sequential and visual-spatial learners possess, as well as strengths and weaknesses of visual-spatials in the charts below.[21]

| The Auditory-Sequential Learner | The Visual-Spatial Learner |
| --- | --- |
| Thinks primarily in words | Thinks primarily in images |
| Has auditory strengths | Has visual strengths |
| Relates well to time | Relates well to space |
| Is a step-by-step learner | Is a whole-part learner |
| Learns by trial and error | Learns concepts all at once |
| Progresses sequentially from easy to difficult material | Learns complex concepts easily; struggles with easy skills |
| Is an analytical thinker | Is a good synthesizer |
| Attends well to details | Sees the big picture; may miss details |
| Follows oral directions well | Reads maps well |
| Does well at arithmetic | Is better at math reasoning than computation |

BEING VISUAL

| The Auditory-Sequential Learner | The Visual-Spatial Learner |
|---|---|
| Learns phonics easily | Learns whole words easily |
| Can sound out spelling words | Must visualize words to spell them |
| Can write quickly and neatly | Much better at keyboarding than handwriting |
| Is well organized | Creates unique methods of organization |
| Can show steps of work easily | Arrives at correct solutions intuitively |
| Excels at rote memorization | Learns best by seeing relationships |
| Has good auditory short-term memory | Has good long-term visual memory |
| May need some repetition to reinforce learning | Learns concepts permanently; does not learn by drill and repetition |
| Learns well from instructions | Develops own methods of problem solving |
| Learns in spite of emotional reactions | Is very sensitive to teachers' attitudes |
| Is comfortable with one right answer | Generates unusual solutions to problems |
| Develops fairly evenly | Develops quite asynchronously |
| Usually maintains high grades | May have very uneven grades |
| Enjoys algebra and chemistry | Enjoys geometry and physics |
| Masters other languages in classes | Masters other languages through immersion |
| Is academically talented | Is creatively, technologically, mechanically, emotionally or spiritually gifted |
| Is an early bloomer | Is a late bloomer |

## Strengths & Weaknesses of the Gifted Visual-Spatial Learner

| Strengths | Weaknesses |
|---|---|
| Thrives on complexity | Poor auditory memory, doesn't remember 3-step instructions |
| Holistic, systems thinker | Difficulty memorizing facts |
| High abstract reasoning ability | Often finds easy work difficult |
| Loves difficult puzzles | Poor at arithmetic |
| Keen visual memory | Has difficulty learning phonics |
| Creative, imaginative | Often has difficulty with spelling unless visualizing |
| Different sense of humor | Difficulty learning mathematical facts |
| Day dreamer-rich fantasy life | Performs poorly or not at all on timed tests |
| Better at mathematical analysis than computation | Easily distracted and can appear inattentive in class |
| Better at reading comprehension than decoding | Disorganized, forgets details |
| Usually better at physics than chemistry | Hates drill and repetition |
| Fascinated by computers, computer graphics | Handwriting labored and difficult to read |
| Avid television watcher | Submits short, sloppy work of poor quality |
| Loves music | Impulsive, tends to act first and think later |
| | "Forgets" written homework assignments |

# I Really Can Draw

I grew up surrounded by art. My mother was a painter, and we made frequent family visits to art museums. Our basement was project central. We were allowed to create anything we wanted from painting, to working with clay, making candles, wood burning, jewelry making and crafting. And, I loved it — the whole family down in that basement, sometimes working on the same project, sometimes doing our own thing.

But everything changed in 6th grade. My art teacher took me aside one day and told me that I had no artistic talent, and I should pursue something other than art. I was devastated. From that moment on, I never picked up another paintbrush or did anything more than doodle on note pads. My only creative outlets were things like hook rugs and craft kits. I never told my mother what my art teacher said. I just stopped going down into the basement and pretended I didn't like it anymore.

Not only did this experience change my life at home, no more family time in the basement, it also affected my choices as I grew older. I didn't feel I was creative enough for many of the careers that appealed to me, such as architecture, so I let myself be directed into general business courses, even considering becoming an attorney. After a couple of decades in the workforce, feeling completely unfulfilled, I made up my mind that I needed to find a different way to make a living. I came across a business, Young Rembrandts, and felt a strong connection. I read Bette Fetter's philosophy that every child can and should be taught how to draw and it resonated with me.

It wasn't long before I found myself in the Young Rembrandts office in Elgin, training as a new franchise owner. And I loved it! As part of training, we were taught several lessons, having the opportunity to draw as our future students would. When I saw the results, I realized my 6th grade art teacher had been completely wrong. I could draw, I really could. I just needed someone to show me how. And, if I could draw, I could paint or sculpt or do anything else I wanted to do. Feeling empowered as an artist once again, brought back childhood memories of those basement projects, and I realized how much I had missed that creative outlet.

On the flight home, I made up my mind that my first stop would be an art supply store. That very same week, I started my first painting in over 30 years. Now, when someone asks if I'm an artist, I say yes.

- Stephanie Black
*Program Director for Young Rembrandts in Orange County, California & former Project Manager for Software Development in the printing industry*

# Teaching
# to the Right

> " My contention is that creativity now is as important in education as literacy, and we should treat it with the same status. "
>
> - Sir Ken Robinson[22]

READING ABOUT LEFT AND RIGHT-BRAIN TRAITS brought fresh insight to many of my own experiences. As I learned about different sides of the brain and their core competencies, it was clear that with my big picture, innovative, relational skills, I'm right-brain dominant. This new understanding gave me language for some of what I felt growing up, but had been unable to articulate. Now I know my skill sets are real. They have value. I don't have to feel bad about not being the other kind of "smart". I'm meant to do and see my way.

It also gave me a greater understanding of what it is to be a visual-spatial student. These kids are having a hard time, but they don't know why. It may be the language, sitting still, testing or memorizing that they struggle with. They know they're not the "same" and they grow tired of feeling like the square peg trying to fit into a round hole. As educators and parents, we can stop the spiral of underachievement and help these kids regain lost confidence. It's critical that our visual students understand the strengths and unique ways their minds work. There are scientific explanations for what may seem to others like a quirky thinking process. Understanding eliminates the question of ability, rebuilds confidence and enables us to focus on developing visual-spatial learning strategies.

These kids need to understand that they see in pictures, and it takes work to translate the volumes of pictures into language. This process takes time, but there are ways to make it a more enjoyable process. It's also natural that their brain rejects drills and memorization styles of learning, preferring to process information simultaneously. Again, it's not because they're wrong, it's because they have other strengths. While there are times they're going to have to memorize and take tests, there are also numerous ways to help our visuals be more successful at home and in the classroom.

## We Need Right & Left

As I have grown and gained understanding of the way I am wired, I have relaxed into myself. I now value being visual, spatial, creative, artistic, spontaneous and relational, but these skills are not enough to operate successfully. It has become increasingly obvious that it's the combination of right AND left-brain skills that have enhanced my abilities. I have been able to be successful in many areas, because I learned to use my left-brain's ability to organize, create structure, include detail and think logically.

Linda Silverman studied gifted students who excelled in visual-spatial portions of IQ tests. She found that gifted, visual-spatial learners showed "extraordinary abilities with visual-spatial tasks, imagistic thinking, complex systems, humor, empathy, music, artistic expression, or creative imagination." Her research has shown that exceptionally gifted students had both visual-spatial and auditory-sequential skills. Students with high visual-spatial skills and weaker auditory-sequential abilities tested poorly, because cognitive tests are designed to test verbal and sequential skills. Silverman also noted that while high scoring, gifted students with both sets of skills tested well, they preferred to use their visual-spatial skills because visual thinking is a powerful, multifaceted mode of thinking. These high scoring students were fortunate, because with both visual-spatial and auditory-sequential strengths, they were able to rely on visual-spatial skills but move back to sequential thinking when needed.

Students without auditory-sequential skills struggle in school systems that are language, linear and test focused. Linda Silverman shares, "The scope and sequence of the curriculum and traditional methods of teaching favor the sequential learner. Auditory-sequential learners are able to show their work easily, because they took a series of steps that they can retrace. They tend to be orderly, well-organized and to follow the sequence of events necessary for high academic performance."[23]

Visual-spatials are not well organized by nature. They can have a hard time at school, because their work lacks logic and sequence. Students without auditory-sequential skills develop low self-esteem, resulting from escalating underachievement, which correlates to their time in the education system.

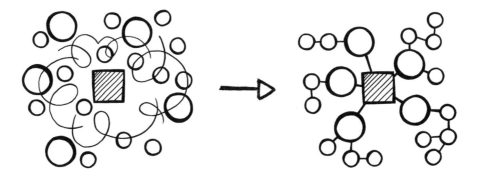

Our visuals need help developing their sequencing and organizational skills. These are not the strengths of visual-spatials. They have their own sense of order and logic, but it's usually not as effective as it needs to be. Organizational and sequencing skills are essential for putting thought into oral and written language. I know for myself, when sharing something I'm passionate and excited about, I have to make a conscious effort to calm my mind and organize my thoughts, or no one will be able to follow my erratic thought process. With so many thoughts happening simultaneously, it takes a lot of effort to arrange them sequentially and speak in whole sentences. Without strong sequencing skills, I would be adrift in my own thoughts, no land in sight. Strengthening organization and sequencing skills will allow our visuals to get what's in their minds out in a logical progression others can comprehend.

## Square Pegs & Round Holes

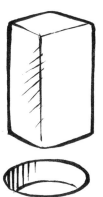

When our children went to elementary school, I experienced an education system struggling to fit square pegs into round holes. After attending Montessori schools through kindergarten, our kids entered the public school system with great success. One of the goals of Montessori education, founded by Maria Montessori in late 1800's, is to help children develop internal order and discipline. We followed the same practices at home, always working to help them learn to organize, complete tasks and think sequentially. All four of our children have strong visual, spatial, relational and conceptual skills, and they all did well in school, but there were times their learning style caused them to be considered the "square peg" to the school system's "round hole".

When our daughter, Emily, transitioned into third grade, we had a fresh revelation on the challenges and labels some visual students face. Our daughter's teacher, "Mrs. Ridge", was an experienced teacher and ran a happy, but challenging, classroom. About mid-year, the students started a project on the animal of their choice. It involved many individual assignments that would be combined into a final report. Our daughter was happy and doing the classroom work well, but there was some confusion as to which assignments were to be completed at home and which to be done in class. One afternoon, I stopped in after school and asked Mrs. Ridge to provide a list of the assignments and designate which were for home and which were for the classroom.

To my surprise this simple request was met with great resistance. The teacher felt an eight-year-old should be able to manage the project on her own and suggested it was time to let her "sink or swim." I disagreed and felt eight-year-olds still need structure and tools to help them learn to manage and organize projects on their own, hence, the list I requested.

Mrs. Ridge would not budge on her point and focused the rest of the conversation on our child's perceived lack of abilities, labeling her "one of those." Not sure what "one of those" was, I asked for clarification. It turned out Mrs. Ridge regarded Emily as the "artistic type" and, "the ones who are too creative for their own good." The teacher saw my daughter as "one of those" that didn't conform and didn't fall easily into line.

I defended artistic types and informed her I was also very visual, artistic, conceptual and operated very successfully in life, as my daughter did in the classroom. Instead of gaining understanding through our dialogue, Mrs. Ridge added my name to the "problem people" category. Eventually, I left the room without the list, without any additional understanding of the third grade assignment, and carrying the blame that "artistic me" had shamefully born another artistic-type which added to the weight of the world.

Directly down the hall was Mrs. Armstrong's classroom, an experienced second grade teacher who had taught several of our kids and had high regard for their abilities. I burst into her room with tears in my eyes, asking "What's wrong with being artistic? What's wrong with my kids?" Dear Mrs. Armstrong assured me there was nothing wrong with any of us and named specific skills and successful traits they demonstrated in the classroom. After further discussion and an explanation of learning styles, she put me at ease about the strengths my children possessed.

Later, as I reconsidered Mrs. Ridge, the third grade teacher, from the perspective of learning styles, I realized she was an orderly, highly structured auditory-sequential, linear thinker. My daughter, a visual-spatial, was a very intelligent child, but her thinking took a more circuitous route as she examined a few more options along the way. This frustrated the teacher. She wanted things done her way, in her time, neat and tidy with little deviation. Many teachers are auditory-sequential, but Mrs. Ridge thought children were right or wrong in relation to her thinking style. She wasn't interested in helping them develop additional skills or adjusting her teaching to match their needs. Few eight-year-olds matched her expectations, and the artistic ones caused her additional challenges.

I later learned that Mrs. Ridge planned her outfits for the week far in advance, carefully matching clothes, jewelry, hair ties and shoes. Every detail was considered and well organized. We visual, relational, creative types also like to accessorize and coordinate our clothing, but tend to be a bit more spontaneous. Both ways work, and we need to be tolerant of our differences.

My own upset had been quelled by understanding that particular teacher's mindset. I wanted our daughter to develop her organizational skills and worked to provide whatever tools I could to bridge the classroom expectations with what she needed to develop. But I also spent the rest of that year with watchful eyes, to protect our creative eight-year-old from becoming frustrated or feeling judged about the nature of her abilities and who she was.

For me, it was really the first time being artistic had been so clearly criticized, considered a detriment in the classroom and as a negative personality trait. Since then, I have heard similar stories from numerous parents and have become increasingly aware of the great divide in learning styles. But I have also become increasingly aware of the unique gifts both styles of learners have to offer and, more importantly, of the *need to develop a balance of abilities in all children.*

## ADD – Distracted or Misunderstood?

There has been a dramatic increase in the diagnoses of ADD and ADHD in our elementary students, yet there is reason to wonder if we are too quick to diagnose and medicate. Are these kids having trouble paying attention, or are they acting out because we're not reaching them?

Attention Deficit Disorder (ADD) is a condition characterized by an inability to concentrate, hyperactivity and impulsive behavior, that affects over 2.5 million children. ADD and ADHD (Attention Deficit Hyperactivity Disorder) diagnoses are on the rise, and prescriptions for Ritalin and similar medications have increased dramatically in recent years. Yet there are concerns that some children are being mislabeled and wrongly medicated, and some debate over what constitutes a true case of ADD and ADHD. According to Jeffery Freed, M.A.T., co-author of *Right-Brained Children in a Left-Brain World: Unlocking the Potential of Your ADD Child,* "ADD is by far the most commonly diagnosed 'psychiatric' problem in children; it accounts for about 50% of child and teen visits to mental health clinics. There is no blood test for Attention Deficit Disorder; children are labeled ADD as the result of a highly subjective evaluation process."

Freed, a private education consultant, goes on to say that while ADD and ADHD genuinely affect 2 to 3% of the population, a small portion of those being diagnosed, there are other explanations for the behaviors being categorized as ADD. After working with over 1000 gifted and ADD children, Freed has come to the conclusion that "most gifted and virtually all children with ADD *share the same learning style.* Simply put, they are all highly visual, non-sequential processors who learn by remembering the way things look and by taking words and turning them into mental pictures. The teaching techniques that work so well for gifted, right-brained students also work with children who have ADD."[24]

> ❝ *The teaching techniques that work so well*
> *for gifted, right-brained students*
> *also work with children who have ADD.* ❞

Educators tend to be left-brain sequential thinkers, with strong organizational and language skills. They did well in school with test taking, linear thinking and memorization. When they see children unable to complete homework assignments, making careless mistakes in schoolwork, having difficulty organizing tasks, having trouble paying attention and displaying impulsive behavior, they may suggest a medical evaluation for ADD, because it can be a way to explain the ill-fitting behaviors. But it's quite normal for visual-spatial children to make careless mistakes in school work, have difficulty organizing, trouble paying attention in language-oriented classrooms, and difficulty sitting still and focusing on linear, language-oriented tasks. Visual-spatial big picture, holistic, spontaneous, relational behaviors can be a contradiction to the conventional classroom structure.

Freed recommends we reconsider the "deficits" of ADD children and look at them through the lens of learning styles. Acknowledging their strengths while making changes to the way we assess, teach and support will enable us to better develop their abilities. The earlier we "intervene with proper teaching techniques" the sooner we embrace their strengths, build self-esteem and enable them to be successful in the classroom.

## Dyslexia

Dyslexia is a learning "disability" with strong ties to visual-spatial learning. Dyslexics think in pictures instead of words, are highly intuitive and think three-dimensionally. Like visual learners, they process language by using mental images. Word images for *cow, dog, run, play* or *stop* are readily available; however, words like *a, the* and *and* do not have corresponding images and cause special challenges for these students. Without the needed images, they grow confused, or disoriented, resulting in reading and learning difficulties. Math, spelling and handwriting are all challenges to the dyslexic because they all involve spoken and written symbols.

The ability to see three-dimensionally can be enormously advantageous, as it is for visual-spatials, but when reading, it can cause dyslexics to become disoriented because words appear to them in a growing number of two and three-dimensional variations. According to Ronald Davis, author of *The Gift of Dyslexia*, "There are at least 40 different variations of a three-letter word such as "cat", and only six of these

are "logical versions", with letters in their correct figurations." To improve reading and learning Davis suggests, "Dyslexics need to form mental pictures they can use to think with, and to associate these pictures visually and auditorily with the words they are trying to learn."[25] Like visual-spatials, dyslexics don't do well with rote learning and need to be involved in making their own mental pictures. Davis's method of helping dyslexic students is to have them create three-dimensional clay models of the words for which they don't have pictures. According to Davis, once they gain the understanding by creating this way, they can use the new symbol to think verbally and nonverbally, and reading improves dramatically.

Alexander Graham Bell, Henry Ford, Walt Disney and many other brilliant minds have been and are dyslexic. *In The Mind's Eye*, by Thomas G. West, examines learning styles of some of the great thinkers of our time, including Thomas Edison, Winston Churchill and Albert Einstein.[26] Their grade school teachers diagnosed them as having learning disorders, because of their visual-spatial behaviors and verbal weaknesses. John Philo Dixon, author of *The Spatial Child*, says, "there are school children who have the potential for understanding the interconnected patterns in quantum theory, quasars, path analysis, thermodynamics, matrix algebra, spatial analysis, etc." Yet, he says they may go unnoticed because some of them "have trouble deciphering *Dick and Jane* in the first grade."[27]

Like visual-spatial students, dyslexic children also have sequencing difficulties. Finding ways to help them develop their ability to order a series of steps is helpful, as is a multisensory approach to education. Math manipulatives, sand paper letters and numbers used in Montessori classrooms, along with other visual, tactile learning supports are critical for these students.

## Why a Picture is Worth a Thousand Words

There are very specific teaching strategies that work well with visual-spatial students. They involve the use of visuals, color, concept, relevancy and drawing. To know how to apply them, we must first understand more about how the visual-spatial learns. Visual learners think in pictures, see in pictures, process, understand and communicate in pictures. Pictures are holistic. They tell the whole story all at once.

Language is more difficult for the visual-spatial thinker, because it's linear and requires progressive, step-by-step processing, requiring extra time when operating in the world of language. Lesley K. Sword, Director of Gifted and Creative Services in Australia, explains how interpreting verbal information into images in order to learn "…requires them to leave reality temporarily in order to do this translating i.e. be unable to hear the current information that is being presented. Once the translation is complete, they return to external reality and continue to switch from taking in external information and closing off external reality in order to translate. The result is that they have a series of

gaps, where they know certain information and miss bits of information. These gaps are especially apparent during review and on tests at school. Also, the translation process takes time, and this means they have difficulty finishing tasks and tests in the time allotted."[28] This also explains their struggle with detail. They've been so busy translating that they missed some things.

Visual thinking is thousands of times faster than language. When visual learners have to rely solely on words to input information, it's a slower and more cumbersome process. It's an incredible undertaking to constantly translate thousands of mental images into linear language. Visual-spatials often struggle to find words for what they can see, or find words as fast as they can think them. It's a time consuming process that left-brain thinkers don't have to deal with and one that right-brain thinkers don't get credit for having to do.

Visual thinkers use their mental imagery to see things it would take thousands of words to describe. Symbolic language is not sufficient for the way visual-spatial minds work. Linda Silverman surmised "Just as the left hemisphere evolved language, a symbolic system surpassing any single sensory modality, perhaps areas in the right hemisphere evolved ways of representing abstractly the two-and three-dimensional relationships of the external world grasped through vision, touch and movement."[29]

## Learning Strategies

Visual kids need to see to learn, so they need time and learning strategies that include making mental pictures of the material they're learning. If the information isn't presented visually, they need to make it visual. To learn and remember, visual learners need to draw pictures, words and phrases to capture information and concepts. When its time to recall learned information, they access the picture memory, often remembering the color, placement on the page and whole words or images to represent concepts.

I draw to learn. Drawing while I listen gives my hands and eyes ways to stay engaged while I receive auditory information. I was excited to learn that research has proven doodling is not the waste of time or inattention teachers told me it was. "Even when listening to an oral presentation, they (visual-spatial students) are likely to be actively creating visual images in order to input and process the information being presented. For them such activities as gazing at the ceiling or out the window or doodling in their notebooks can actually assist in their learning."[30] Drawing while I listen keeps me involved.

I also use color to create visual information I can remember, which explains my deep affection for the rainbow of ultra-fine point sharpie markers I keep close at hand. As a college student, I learned to study visually. I did it intuitively, but now I do it intentionally. My notes often include arrows, stars and symbols to represent concepts. When trying to recall information learned, I remember the picture of the whole word, the colored image and where it was on the page.

To learn to spell, education consultant Jeffery Freed suggests students first write the words in color, because color is an aid to retention. Researchers have shown that the use of color with instruction stimulus increases performance. Once written, he recommends the child take a mental snapshot of the word image and of what it represents. Being intentional about memorizing pictures of words and their meaning is critical. For more advanced words, he suggests writing the word using different colors for each syllable, increasing the value of the picture memory. This same strategy can be used in a variety of ways, but the key is having students make or find colorful images to remember.

Right-brain, visual-spatials are conceptual thinkers, who learn information all at once. Lesley K. Sword shares, "Whereas left-brain thinking is step-by-step, linear thinking over time, right-brain thinking is a holistic system where all knowledge is interconnected in space."[31] Visual thinkers assimilate information best when it's presented conceptually, within a context and related to other concepts. Once they grasp the information and see how it relates to other stored data, creating mental pictures in the process, their learning is permanent. They have poor auditory short-term memory, but excel in long-term memory, so drill and memorization styles of learning are ineffective and even painful for them. Because they learn holistically, their learning is a network of relationships. Information also requires relevance.

> " *Visual thinkers assimilate information best when it's presented conceptually, within a context and related to other concepts.* "

Visual-spatials need to know why the information matters, understand it as it relates to the larger whole, and then create ways to see and connect it. Then when they get it, they get it for the long term. Understanding the why, the concept behind the data or computation is critical to their success.

## Handwriting

Visual-spatials are usually described as having poor handwriting skills. Being artistic, I have lovely handwriting — when I want to. But my hands don't move as fast as I think, and my writing often looks less than lovely. Keyboarding is on the rise, and handwriting, specifically cursive, is taught less and less in schools. Computer keyboards do provide the speed and kinesthetic activity many desire, but as a visual-spatial thinker, I cannot imagine my world without the ability to write, verbally or visually. Writing is essential to my thinking and communication.

More than forty states in the U.S. have eliminated cursive from the current education curriculum. Since it is no longer required and is not part of standardized testing, classroom instruction time is being redirected to other test related subject matter. Other arguments for its demise point to the need for keyboarding skills as students advance to higher levels of learning. Yet, according to publishers of educational writing materials, more than 80% of written classroom work is still done by hand.[32]

There are numerous research studies that demonstrate the physical act of writing actually helps children process learning on a deeper cognitive level. A 2010 study by University of Washington researcher Virginia Berninger found, after testing students in grades 2, 4 and 6, that elementary students actually wrote faster by hand than keyboard and they generated more ideas while writing.[33] There is also evidence that the sequential finger movements used in writing activate regions of the brain used in learning and memory. The physical act of writing integrates auditory, visual, physical and oral processes while learning. Another study, from Indiana University, demonstrated that children who practiced writing by hand had increased neural activity compared to children who learned by looking at letters.[34]

Mastery of the physical act of writing, especially cursive, builds a level of unconscious competence for the learner. This  competence means writing will require less attention and allow students to focus on content. "Since so many right-brained children have fine motor difficulties, the very act of writing requires tremendous concentration, which takes away from the ability to focus on the task at hand. When children write, it's more difficult for them to visualize because they are looking down at the page trying to remember how to spell and how to form the letters of the words."[35] Helping them gain mastery in fine motor skills will empower them as they approach yet another burdensome interaction with words.

Visual-spatial kids may also struggle with writing sequentially. Freed, in explaining the difference for the visual-spatial kid, says, "his multidimensional visual orientation also makes him more prone to errors in copying letters and numbers; he may reverse them or write entire words backwards."[36] Cursive is a more effective method of writing because, unlike printing, the letters are connected. Visual kids learn by writing and remember by "seeing" the words they wrote. Cursive engages them in the process of making the words and creates whole words they can remember.

Handwriting is functional, but also a reflection of who we are. Betty Edwards, author of *Drawing on the Right Side of the Brain*, shares, "In all the ways we express

ourselves nonverbally, none is quite so personal as our handwriting — so personal and important that our signatures are legally protected as a mark of identity. Unlike other ways we express individuality, we have sole ownership of our handwriting. It is a personal possession that no other person is allowed to use or imitate." Betty Edwards teaches non-artistic adults the value of using the right side of their brain. When working with them she asked, " 'How many of you want to improve your handwriting?' Nearly all the hands go up. If I ask 'Why?' the answers vary; 'I want my handwriting to look better…. To be more readable….to be good enough to be proud of.' "[37]

As much as computer competency is becoming essential, right *and* left-brain individuals still need to know how to put pencil to paper and write what they want to write. And as much as we need to know how to write, someone else is going to have to be able to read what we write.

## Visual Organizers

While writing and note taking is never going to be natural for visual-spatials, the ability to record and organize thought is essential. This skill is expected to develop naturally over time, but our visuals need some special help. Auditory-sequential students are more at ease with the writing and note taking process, since they are more sequential by nature and don't require the visualization. But our simultaneous learners with less affinity for linear thinking can be overwhelmed. It's critical our visual-spatials know how to get their thoughts on paper, how to organize a paper and use a calendar, but it's going to take some special attention and may require some unique tools.

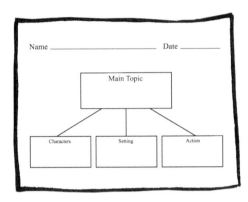

Many elementary teachers are using graphic organizers in their classrooms. These tools are designed to help children capture information and organize their thoughts in a visual format. While these tools benefit all students, they're essential for our visuals and helpful long after elementary school. There are plenty of visual-spatial students struggling in high school and college, even avoiding classes that might be too text-heavy or language-driven. They're bright and have much to say and share, but it's our responsibility to give them tools to help them organize the incoming verbal data. Graphic organizers can also help get their divergent thoughts and image based ideas on paper.

Educators can provide tools that adapt and grow with our students from early childhood into college. More sophisticated visual organizers can help high school and college students record information and organize their thoughts. Mind mapping, the process of taking notes visually, allows the visual learner to create their own organizational structure. Mind maps usually include the use of color and drawn symbols and help the learner classify information and visualize ideas. Mind mapping and graphic organizers can also be used as an aid to study, solve problems or structure writing assignments. Computer programs are now available for these same tasks, and some even transfer the data into outline form as an aid in more complex writing assignments.

Technology is providing new opportunities to be visual in business and the classroom with the introduction of smartboards. These interactive white boards allow teachers and business leaders to project websites, images and videos to create colorful, engaging presentations that appeal to both visual and auditory learners. They also allow the user to manipulate the content on the screen with the touch of a finger, making the learning experience dynamic and interactive. The use and success of these tools in the business world remind us that visual-spatial needs stay with us long past grade school.

## Writing with Visual Tools

Our son, Matt, is a visual, kinesthetic learner, so on large, text heavy assignments we implemented tools to make the process match his learning style. In high school, Matt was assigned a twelve page paper titled "The American Character." Students had to identify a characteristic they felt represented Americans, such as freedom, independence and perseverance. They found examples in literature, historic events and pop culture to illustrate the characteristic within three different time periods.

Matt was interested in the subject matter, but overwhelmed organizing the multifaceted assignment, so we decided to make it visual and tactile. We cleared off the dining room table, pulled out graphic organizers and small sticky notes and proceeded to establish a physical system for organizing the project. Graphic organizers are designed to help visual

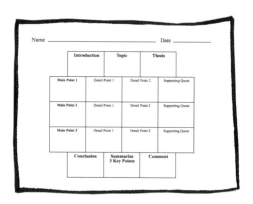

students organize and categorize their thoughts. The one we used was specifically designed to help older students write complex papers and speeches. The 8 1/2 x 11 inch piece of paper was full of carefully planned spaces, organized for the paragraphs and supporting details needed for written work.

Matt's writing assignment was essentially three papers in one, with three key components within each paper, so we laid it out exactly that way on the dining room table. There were three rows of graphic organizers, one for each time period. In each row (time period) we laid out three more organizers, one for each way he needed to illustrate the characteristic — through history, literature and pop culture. Each organizer contained three rows of small squares where he could plan his key points, quotes and examples. Instead of writing directly on the organizers, I gave him small sticky notes that matched the size of the individual squares. Writing on the small pieces of paper and then placing them on the organizer gave him the freedom and opportunity to physically organize and arrange his thoughts as he researched and experienced them. This flexibility also made the process less intimidating. We added one more organizer for the introduction of the paper, as well as one for the concluding thoughts.

With the organization of the paper so visual, Matt was able to see the project as a whole, and see the individual components as well. The physical layout of the paper was also helpful for him as a kinesthetic learner, as he moved back and forth to physically touch and move the papers while he used them. Once he decided on the characteristic he would use as his theme and the three time periods, he was able to work on individual sections one at a time, clearly understanding how they related back to the whole. After all his research and planning was completed on the organizers, he took one organizer at a time off the table and headed to the computer to write up that section of the paper. To maintain the physical order of the paper visual, he carefully placed each organizer back on the table until the paper was complete. Once all the writing was complete, he reviewed the whole paper several times to add transition sentences and final edits.

Matt completed the assignment very successfully and was even able to enjoy the process because we had adapted it. What could have been an overwhelming and frustrating experience became completely reasonable when it was made visual, tactile and physical.

## Compositional Writing

Translating thoughts into written form is challenging for us visual-spatials. For us, language is slower and less dynamic, requiring time and mental activity to translate our rich multidimensional images into linear language. For me, writing this book has been a laborious process of sifting through piles and piles of thought, prioritizing and then sequencing them in

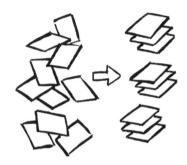

order to share in language. I literally see different groups of concurrent thoughts going on in my brain and see myself choosing the concepts I want to translate to words, struggling to order and stack them like cards. It's frustrating. Exhausting. I can see it. I get it. I know what I want to say. I see the conclusion to my thinking, the answer to my inner query, but proving how I got there and showing my work doesn't come naturally to me. It's a completely different process for me to explain myself. It makes me feel strangely inadequate, but it helps to know it's "normal". It's not about me. It's just my mind switching from my natural operating system to a slower, less comfortable one. It takes more effort, but it can be done.

Visual thinkers can have a difficult time writing because their visual skills are in direct contrast to the skills needed to write effectively. Gerald Grow, in "The Writing Problems of Visual Thinkers," attributes the difficulties to three key areas: "a lack of words, unfamiliarity with the kind of analysis that leads to logical sequencing of prose and difficulty understanding that context must be communicated."[38]

Visual thinkers see pictures and can have difficulty translating their rich images into words. Their words can be imprecise, too broad and even cryptic. Visuals don't have the same vocabulary auditory-sequential thinkers have. *We* live in the world of images. *They* live in words. But writing requires words. We visual-spatials need some help finding our words.

"Semantic memory is the memory for use in language. It is a mental thesaurus, organized knowledge a person possesses about words and other symbols, their meaning and referents, about relations among them, about rules, formulas and algorithms for the manipulation of these symbols, concepts and relations."[39] Visual-spatials have this type of picture memory, but it's full of visual images and spatial relationships, not words. This is another place we need some help!

> ❝ *Visual thinkers see pictures and can have difficulty translating their rich images into words.* ❞

Writing requires the ability to sequence a series of thoughts in order to tell a story or explain a position. Visuals think simultaneously, holistically and may not have the sequencing skills needed to separate and organize their thoughts effectively. This lack of sequencing and order in writing leads to scattered, poorly organized material and enormous frustration for both the reader and the writer.

Visuals are big picture thinkers. They see and understand all at once. When writing, they may not understand the need to explain the context, use comparisons, give supporting detail and show how they arrived at their conclusions. Grow describes the writing of a visual as "a map of all possibilities; a verbal thinker writes like a guided tour."[40] We need to help our visuals get their maps and rich imagery onto paper, sequentially. We are often focused on their problems with grammar, but in reality it's about helping them find the right words, organize their content and create context. The more we understand their underlying thought processes, the better we can teach them.

## Improving the Dreaded Essay

I recently met a teacher who was retired from classroom teaching and now acts as a private tutor for elementary kids. After a lively discussion about what we perceived to be challenges of visual students, she shared her strategies for teaching young children to write. Using the example of that dreaded fall essay, "What I did on my summer vacation," she talked about the ways she helps children prepare for

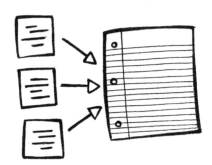

writing assignments. She began the assignment by explaining the context of the paper they would write, how long it would be and what kinds of things they could write about. To begin writing, she stirred up memories by talking about summer and the kinds of activities they may have participated in. She asked questions,

such as, did they go out of town? Did they go swimming, visit family or attend a camp? In response, they talked about who they spent time with, where they were and how they felt.

Next, they made lists on paper, starting with nouns, naming places they went and people who were with them. Then verbs — running, swimming, driving and playing, followed by adjectives and adverbs — hot, wet, cold, scared, fun and fast. After the lists were made, she explained more about the structure of the essay and with memories activated and lists of words to describe, they were ready to write. She found that by being proactive in explaining context, walking them through the process and helping them find their words in advance, they were much less intimidated, moved to action quicker and were more successful overall.

## Visual-Spatial Math

There are brilliant, spatially gifted kids underachieving in math, and their low computation scores embarrass them. They're often shamed, misunderstood and even ridiculed, because they're bored and may be thinking beyond the assessment. They don't understand what's wrong and will assume it's them. But it's not about the student, it's about the misdiagnoses of the problem and our teaching methods.

Success in math is based on computation skills, repetition and timed tests, all negatives for right-brain thinkers. Visual-spatials can be highly gifted in math and reasoning abilities, but their ability can go unnoticed because of careless computation mistakes. But visuals with strong spatial abilities have the ability to understand and visualize complex mathematical concepts, even while making simple computation errors.

To teach math effectively, highly spatial kids need to first understand relevancy and the concept behind the computation. Share the big picture. Tell them why it matters and how it fits into the whole. This increases relevancy, engages them and increases opportunities for success. Teaching concepts behind computation is not just for our visual-spatial students. When teaching is focused heavily on computation and fact memorization, there is a risk that all learners will miss the underlying mathematical concepts.

There are many ways to make math more interesting for everyone in the classroom; use manipulatives, add images, make number games, board games, play math games, use familiar objects, incorporate movement and make it fun. Use real life situations. Make it conceptual, visual, tactile, kinesthetic. Then compute.

## Teaching Math Conceptually

As an experienced 7th grade math teacher, I teach many topics like fractions, decimals, exponents and roots, ratios, percents, geometry, probability, data and statistics, which have been introduced during a student's elementary years. While it's helpful when students have some familiarity with these topics, if computation has been taught without a full understanding of the concept behind it, I find students have difficulty moving forward. After 21 years of teaching math at various grade levels, I have found students are much more successful when math is first taught conceptually and then taught the procedural number crunching associated with that concept. Students are able to move on to more advanced math application and concepts when they have a solid conceptual foundation. When this process is reversed and students learn computation without theory, it is extremely difficult for them to go back and grasp the conceptual meaning later. For example, almost every student I have ever taught felt inadequate working with fractions, because a strong conceptual base was not established before learning all the "rules" of adding, subtracting, multiplying and dividing fractions.

One of my favorite concepts to teach is the Pythagorean Theorem. It is a brand new topic and students have no prior experience, hence no misconceptions to correct. When teaching math concepts, I use a highly visual tactile approach. I have found this essential to my students' understanding. I also feel they are more engaged and the learning "sticks". Once students visually understand the Pythagorean Theorem,

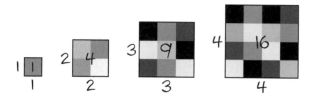

they make fewer computation errors. Conversely, a colleague who taught the Pythagorean Theorem formula first without a visual picture, noticed his students making errors because they didn't understand the underlying theory. He tried to go back and teach the visual representation, but it seemed to just confuse his students. Another colleague, a special education teacher, introduced the theory conceptually and visually, as

I did, and had tremendous success when the students later used the formula to compute.

Before introducing the Pythagorean Theorem, I must be sure students understand square numbers. To do this, each student receives a bag of colored 1-inch square tiles, and are told to make a square with the tiles. As I roam around the room, I see students who have selected one tile, others who have created a 2x2 square, a 3x3 square, etc. But surprisingly, I also see students who have created a variety of rectangles. After posing questions to help students remember the attributes of a square, they make the needed adjustments and soon all students have illustrated a square. As students share their squares with their classmates, we discuss the areas of their squares: $2^2$ or 4 tiles, $3^2$ or 9 tiles, $4^2$ or 16 tiles, etc. When I explain to the students that they have created a

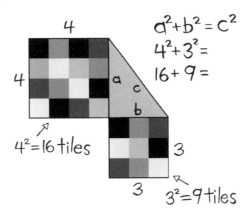

visual representation of a square number using the colored squares, it is a light bulb moment. For years, they have heard "two squared, three squared, etc.," but they hadn't made the connection between the words and a visual picture!

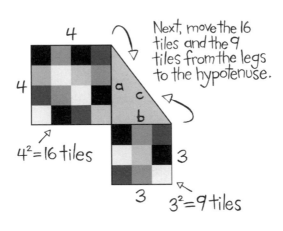

With this understanding of squares, they're ready to apply the concept of square numbers to the Pythagorean Theorem. To do this, every student receives a right triangle with legs that are 4 inches and 3 inches long with the task of trying to determine the length of the third side called the hypotenuse. This is the first time that the students are introduced to the Pythagorean Theorem formula: $a^2 + b^2 = c^2$. I ask the students to illustrate $a^2$ and $b^2$ using the square tiles. They use 16 square tiles to make a square off the 4-inch leg, and 9 square tiles to make a square off the 3-inch leg.

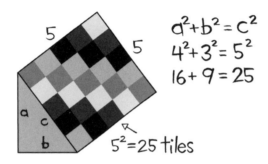

$$a^2 + b^2 = c^2$$
$$4^2 + 3^2 = 5^2$$
$$16 + 9 = 25$$

$5^2 = 25$ tiles

The students then realize that if $a^2 + b^2 = c^2$, they can prove it is true by moving the 16 tiles from one leg and the 9 tiles from the other leg to create the square on the third side of the right triangle, which is called the hypotenuse.

When the 16 square tiles from one leg and the 9 square tiles from the other leg are moved to the third side, or hypotenuse, the 25 total tiles makes a 5x5 square. Therefore, the students have just visually proved that the sum of the squares of the two legs of a right triangle equals the square of the hypotenuse.

I have always had great success with this lesson and other visual, conceptual math lessons. I have found conceptual learning is enormously facilitated by visual tactile learning strategies and children are more successful when conceptual understanding precedes computation.

-Lynn Pittner
*7th grade math teacher at Central Middle School in California,*
*& currently in her 22nd year of teaching*

## Chocolate Math

As an adult pursuing my master's in Business Administration, I had first-hand experience of using visuals in a language-oriented, numeric computation class. It was Qualitative Analysis for Decision Makers, taught by a highly energetic, passionate professor who spoke fluent statistics. On the first day of class, I was completely overwhelmed by the new vocabulary, the calculation requirements and computer graphing assignments. I was out of my element, but as an adult, I was more aware of what the problems were. Determined to do whatever it took, I found a helpful tutor, drew lots of visual charts and pictures to illustrate concepts, learned, with much assistance, how to create graphs in Excel, and met with the instructor as needed.

What began as an overwhelming disaster became a very satisfying class, because the professor was highly committed to each person's success and was willing to make adjustments to her own teaching style. She also used visual and tactile experiences to help us understand concepts before we spent time calculating. I vividly remember the day she came into class, with large bags of chocolate M&M candy and small paper cups. She proceeded to pass out small cups of candy to each student and we sorted, divided, counted and ate candy as she taught variance, means, range and deviations in groups of data.

This was so much better than more stats talk and another diagram on the chalkboard. I understood and remembered the information because of the visual, multisensory, concept oriented exercise. At my age, I can force myself to stay engaged to learn the material, but the visual, big picture concept and relevancy she conveyed made the subject much more enjoyable. The shift in language was also a huge help, as she adjusted her fluent statistical lingo to speak color and M&M. Understanding concepts in language we are familiar with, both verbal and visual, helps us gain understanding before we transition to specific subject matter prose.

## Making it Visual at Home

Being visual, I was always drawn to ways of making my own kids' world more visual. To help organize their dressers, I drew simple pictures of the type of clothes in each drawer and attached them to the front of the corresponding drawer. The simple image of a sock, underwear, short sleeve shirt or pants helped maintain order and enabled them to find their clothes easily and operate more independently. As they grew older and were able to put clean laundry back into the dresser, they could easily follow the visual organizational system.

When kids first learn to put on their own shoes, they struggle with getting the correct shoe on each foot. To help them be successful and independent, we added dots where the inside soles came together. They put the shoes on the floor, carefully matching the dots and when they could match them, they were then aligned properly and could put them on their feet correctly.

To help my pre-schoolers organize activity, I made very short lists using only images. Their bedtime routine was a series of colorful pictures; a pair of pajamas (to put on), a pair of hands (to wash), a toothbrush and toothpaste, and a book (to read after everything else was complete). As they got older, the lists became more complex, but I was mindful to keep them as simple as possible and not to use too much language. When it came time for organizing family activities or sending kids to do their chores, a flood of words and directions frustrated and confused them. We were more successful when I took the time to write individual lists, minimizing the number of words while adding visuals, humor and creativity to the task at hand. The kids took their lists, managed their own projects and felt the satisfaction of crossing things off when completed.

## Walgreens Goes Visual

The use of visuals to improve communication and understanding affects people from infancy to adulthood. Using visuals to communicate improves performance in school, at home and in business. In 2007, in an effort to hire a significant number of employees with disabilities, Walgreens opened a distribution facility designed to accommodate the learning and communication needs of the disabled community. One of Walgreens' top executives, Randy Lewis, has a son with autism. His child's special education needs enabled him to better understand the needs of his new workers, and he applied his insight to the redesign of the facility. Lewis knew this group "didn't learn the way we're used to teaching," so when it came time for designing a facility that would serve this community, they used

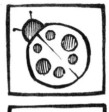

increased visuals, touch screens instead of keyboards and images that related tasks to corresponding departments. Their goal was to make the facility fully functional for employees with and without disabilities.

The distribution center in Anderson, South Carolina includes employees with physical and cognitive disabilities ranging from autism and Down syndrome to the visual and hearing impaired. While 40% of their 700 employees are considered disabled, all 700 workers operate in this highly visual facility that includes automated guided vehicles, adjustable workstations and a redesigned, easier to use computer interface.

Workstations are marked by a number and objects such as ladybugs, dogs and turtles. The transportation department uses images of trains, wagons and trucks. Workstations are also equipped with a monitor that lights up as it measures productivity levels. Green signals meeting and exceeding; red indicates rates below standard. Visual signals provide feedback on performance and allow employees to adjust work speeds.

Management found the facility design resulted in a 20% gain in productivity and made work easier for all employees, claiming, "we found the improvements actually benefit all distribution center employees, the result is a workplace that's friendlier to all of its employees."[41]

## Learning to Be Quiet

We need to expose children to periods of silence and involve them in activities where quiet is pleasurable, so they learn to enjoy the comfort of quiet contemplation. The world continues to grow increasingly busy with cell phones, televisions, computers and an array of hand held devices to amuse and distract us. It would benefit us all, children and adults, to turn off and tune out from time to time and experience silence. Being intentional about pursuing the sound of our own thoughts is key to cultivating innovation and creativity. Einstein, da Vinci and Edison had consistent streams of ideas running through their minds, but those thoughts required cultivation and listening time.

For me, art, sewing, embroidery, baking, making and building satisfied my need to create. But these independent, peaceful pursuits also cultivated the joy of silence and the pleasure of spending time in my own quiet thoughts. Today's kids are bombarded by stimuli from a variety of sources — television, computers and video games — as well as an ever-increasing amount of time spent in team sports or group activity. Yet they are lacking in time spent being quiet. They're missing the joy of silence and delight of independent activity.

The first time I experienced being intentional about quieting my body and mind was in high school. But it was in gym, not art class. Instead of learning yet another sport, we stopped moving and learned to be still and control our thoughts. This was especially significant for us as teenagers, our bodies, minds and emotions in a constant state of angst or celebration. Our young, less traditional gym teacher had been a professional dancer and often took us to the dance studio for some "alternative" gym exercises. I looked forward to these days, wondering what new experiences she would share with us.

These alternative activities had a profound effect on me. My favorite was our "relaxation exercises". Our assignment was to envision ourselves as rag dolls. We lay on the studio floor, lights dimmed, music playing softly in the background, and we learned to be quiet. With a calm soothing voice, our teacher walked quietly around the room and described sand leaking out of our ragdoll bodies. As she talked, she created visual images that enabled us to "see" the sand leaving different parts of our bodies, allowing us to release muscle tension and melt into the floor

quiet

beneath us. As we listened and followed her instruction, from our head to our toes, we relaxed. First we loosened the muscles in our faces. We cleared our minds, loosened our shoulders, stomachs, hips and legs, until the last bit of sand drained

2

out our toes. Once empty, we became aware of silence and the sound of our breath. Once empty of the busyness of the day and our inner chatter, we were able to choose what thoughts we wanted to think, see what we wanted to see. This ability to clear my mind and calm my body was very impactful, and later, as an adult, I sought out ways to repeat the experience.

## Supermom Needs to Relax & Visualize

In my early efforts to be Supermom, I decided to go through labor and delivery of my first child without pain medication. I was sure I could make it through anything for the good of my unborn child. When labor started, I reaffirmed my conviction and set myself to endure. Midway through labor, I understood just how incredibly intense labor pains really are and changed my mind, asking for pain relief — any relief. Labor was too far along for an epidural, requiring me to follow through with my no pain medication plan. Miraculously and without tearing the room or my dear husband apart, our daughter was born. I made it — thankful for a remarkably short, six-hour labor time overall.

Two and a half years later, I had somehow managed to forget the intensity of labor and was back in the delivery room for another natural, no medication delivery. The reality of intense pain came even sooner, but being as stubborn as I am, I was still sure I could manage it. As each contraction came, I resisted the pain and unfortunately that resistance made me, baby, and others miserable and lengthened the labor process significantly. Twenty-four hours later, our second daughter was born.

Between baby two and baby three, I stumbled across relaxation and visualization classes. Remembering my high school experience and thinking they would help me creatively, I enrolled. Week after week, the instructor led us through exercises designed to help us learn to quiet ourselves. Once quiet, we learned to call forth memories, rich with detail, to imagine new places and to "see" with our mind's eye.

We learned to quiet our bodies and still our inner chatter so that we could *use* our mind to do what we wanted it to do. For the first time since high school, I relaxed. I could truly quiet my whole self completely. Week after week, I continued to train, eventually noticing I was calmer, internally and externally. I could control the way my mind often raced or moved off track and could now purposefully direct my thoughts and inner queries. This newfound power over my own mind excited me and impacted many areas of my life. I had always been active, always in motion and would certainly have been diagnosed as ADD if they had been testing for it back then. Finally, I could control my mind. I was master over myself.

A year later, I was headed back to labor and delivery for the third time. I brought this newfound mental discipline into the birthing room with me, not sure what to expect. Once again, I wanted a drug-free delivery. But this time, because of my ability to control my response to physical stimuli, husband, baby and I went through what was a remarkably peaceful labor and delivery. For the birth of our fourth child, three years later, it was an even more profound experience. Now that I knew what was possible, I prepared by practicing delivery related visualizations. Once in the birthing room, I kept my eyes closed and controlled my breathing as I fought to maintain my concentration. I focused on seeing the waves of pain as positive sensations preparing my body to deliver. Hours passed, and labor progressed beautifully. Eventually, thinking I had fallen asleep, the doctor whispered in my ear, "Do you want to push?" I carefully opened my right eye, looked directly at the doctor and said, "YES!" Moments later, our son arrived. My doctor commented later on how "lucky" I was, but I knew the entire experience had been a remarkable testament to the power we have to harness and direct our mind and thoughts.

Aside from transforming the experience of childbirth, the ability to quiet myself, visualize and tune out the world has been a tremendous aid to me in art and business. Organizing my thought process, observing patterns and developing fresh insight comes more easily when I push the busyness aside and think in a clear space. It also allows me to focus my thought process, develop new ideas, connect disparate thoughts and think innovatively. As I have matured in my faith, this ability has also enabled me to reach new heights and depths spiritually. During times of worship, extended prayer and reflection, it allows me to hear my own thoughts and inner query. Most importantly, it allows me to step away from myself and into the presence of God. When I am free to listen, I feel His affection, hear His truth, His direction and His words of encouragement.

## It's About Balance

More art, more visuals and more creative development are good news for us right-brained, visual-spatials. It's time our abilities are valued, appreciated and even sought after. BUT, and this is a very big BUT, *being right-brained is not enough!* We must also be mindful to develop the auditory-sequential skills of our left-brain. While the visual-spatial, big picture, relational, creative, less detail-oriented people bring a lot to the table, it's going to require language, organizational skills and the ability to think sequentially and logically to get all those great ideas out of our heads and onto paper. Mathematicians and scientists need to prove their work. Technology innovators and engineers must be able to build what they imagine.

Right ⊕ left

As we adapt teaching methods to address the needs of visual kids, we must not let the pendulum swing too far to the right. To operate successfully, we must have a healthy balance of abilities. Our goal is not to raise a generation of undisciplined, free-spirited artsy types that cannot organize or manage themselves. Children need to grow up using their innate processing modes, while at the same time developing the less dominant parts of their brain needed to be successful. We are being tasked to develop creative, innovative minds that can meet deadlines, think logically, communicate effectively and get done what needs to get done. As educators, it's imperative we prepare children for a future that embraces linear <u>and</u> non-linear thinking, text <u>and</u> context, logic <u>and</u> intuition.

## Creativity & Innovation

Sir Ken Robinson, author and international consultant on creativity and innovation in business and education, sees creativity as essential to shaping the future. Robinson shared, "My contention is that creativity now is as important in education as literacy, and we should treat it with the same status." If creativity is essential to shaping our future, we need to be sure we have a 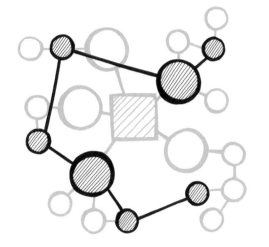 clear understanding of its meaning. According to Merriam-Webster's dictionary, creativity is "artistic or intellectual inventiveness" and "the skill and imagination to create new things."[42] Creativity is not, and has never been, limited to the arts and it's not reflected by one's ability to do art. Creativity comes in many forms. Creativity is a way of thinking. It's a thought process of which we're all capable.

Steve Jobs, one of the most creative minds of the twentieth century, once said, "Creativity is just connecting things. When you ask creative people how they did something, they feel a little guilty because they didn't really do it, they just saw something. It seemed obvious to them after a while. That's because they were able to connect experiences they've had and synthesize new things."[43]

To create, we need to be aware of ***what is*** and ***what has been***. Then we think about ***what else***? What else can be? What else can we do? What else can we make? Creativity is the ***what next***? Creativity requires us to apply original thought in order to arrive at new possibilities. But we can't just think it. Turning what we can imagine into reality requires doing. Creating requires action — *doing*. Doing requires logical, sequential thought and activity. Creating and doing is where right meets left.

> " *Creativity is just connecting things. When you ask creative people how they did something, they feel a little guilty because they didn't really do it, they just saw something. It seemed obvious to them after a while. That's because they were able to connect experiences they've had and synthesize new things.* " — Steve Jobs

Steve Jobs was very good at the *what else, what next*. But he was also a master of doing. As a brilliant innovator, he knew how to turn ideas into products and services that changed the way we work, play and communicate on a global level. According to Merriam-Webster's dictionary, innovation is the process of "introducing something new," a "new method, idea or device."[44] Creativity is the idea. Innovation is when business or organizations turn those ideas into useful products, services or business practices.

Creative, imaginative thought comes easily for young children. They're driven to discover and understand *what is*. They delight in imagining *what can be*. Once they get to school, we ask their imaginations to take a backseat while we develop their logic and linear thinking skills. In the process of being so logical and linear, they may be robbed of their creative power. Their confidence and ability to bring *what else* into the thought process may be weakened or even lost. It doesn't have to be this way. When we educate both the right and left, we educate the creative and the logical.

The arts are subjects that have value in and of themselves, but they are also the subjects that develop creative thinking, multiple solutions and new insights.

Bring the arts back into the classroom and, as Robinson said, "treat them with the same status."[45] BUT we need to teach them in ways that are intentional about fully developing right-brain visual strengths, WHILE acquiring sequential, logical thought processes and skill sets. With this preparation, we can raise a generation of creative innovators with disciplined minds that have the skills needed to affect change on a global level.

## Being Soft on Artists

When our daughters were in high school, our school district created academies within the four area high schools. Each academy had an area of focus: technology, foreign language, science and fine arts. Our high school housed the Fine Arts Academy. Fifty students a year were accepted and attended classes in their specialty of art, music, dance or theater, along with general education classes. While I was excited about the arts receiving this attention and focused development, I was often concerned by the way some of the staff regarded the artistic students in their care. Some of the drama department staff felt we couldn't or shouldn't expect the creative students to work the same way the other students did. Unfortunately "not the same" often translated to "not as hard" as other students. Recognizing these artistic students thought and operated differently was great, but being creative or visual-spatial doesn't mean they don't have to work as hard.

Honoring creative abilities is not an excuse for underperformance. These academy theater classes were unstructured and open-ended, with few requirements, skill-specific goals or measurements. The students were required to perform in a variety of productions along with the opportunity to volunteer on different production committees. However, they were often left to emote, create, and consider without any real goal or purpose. The problem seemed to stem from the top down, because the drama teachers operated this way themselves.

The more driven and structured students were often frustrated. The lax attitude had filtered into some of the academic classes. Some students opted out of Fine Arts Academy, knowing they needed more structure and expectation to prepare them for college.

I remember thinking that these art academy students weren't being prepared for life after school and certainly not being prepared for life as a theater professional. Being professional actors, dancers, directors or designers are highly demanding and competitive careers. All students, both visual and linear thinkers, need to work hard, acquire skills and deliver results in order to be successful in their chosen career.

Every member of our family is a visual, artistic, creative and conceptual thinker. Our home was a constant whirlwind of creative energy. Our kids were always making, building, sewing or inventing something. They even played spatially, with each one participating in a variety of sports, music lessons, dance, art and theater. And while we were intentional about them having so many creative and physical outlets, we were also mindful to create a structured environment. Their minds were free to enjoy and explore, but there were timelines and expectations, and we looked for ways to develop the internal order, structure and discipline that life requires.

## Right without Enough Left

Like their parents, our visual-spatial children participated in music and theater. Our three daughters enjoyed performing, and our son was more interested in set design and construction. As a family, we were fortunate to be involved in a local children's theater group that staged three productions a year. Each show involved 70 to 120 children between seven and fifteen years old, with older students advancing to the high school/junior college ensemble for two shows a year. As a participatory ensemble of the community college, we used high caliber theater facilities. Parent volunteers provided much of the necessary labor, and our budgets often allowed us to hire professional artists for stage, costume and lighting design, as well as music, dance and acting directors.

The purpose of this group was to give children, as many children as possible, the opportunity to experience and participate in theater. Memorizing lines or songs, learning to dance and sing, being on stage in front of crowds and being part of an ensemble were rich, multisensory activities that blessed our children in numerous ways. Rehearsals, practice, repetition and expectation further enhanced their value. A small minority of the children went on to professional theater careers. The majority formed deep friendships, gained confidence and had experiences that were critical to their development.

I began my fourteen-year association with this group first as a parent volunteer painting sets and sewing costumes. Eventually, I assembled and led production teams, hired designers and had a place on the Board of Directors. Participating in this group offered me endless opportunities to use and expand my art skills, develop my leadership abilities and work alongside wonderful men and women with a passion for the arts and service to their community. As a volunteer worker, I felt the first-hand effects of working with different designers. Later, as an organizer, I made hiring decisions based on my experience working with those designers.

Time spent with this group gave me first-hand understanding about why it was essential for right-brain people to develop their left-brain capabilities. One of my first volunteer assignments had me painting sets for a very talented designer. "Sam" was enormously talented, but lacked organization and communication skills, seriously affecting our production teams and performers. He created stunning backdrops and three-dimensional scenery. His artistic talent was greatly admired and brought a heightened level of professionalism to our troupe of young actors.

As painters, we were honored to paint the designs he drew. After we completed the basic painting, he came along adding shadows, textures and details to heighten the sense of realism. Throughout the set painting process, there had always been areas of confusion with a lack of clear direction and communication. While we admired his talent and creations, the closer we got to opening night, the more the stress level escalated. As opening night approached, there was still much to be painted and many details left incomplete.

For this show, Sam created a wonderful three-dimensional shoe, ten feet by fourteen feet. The design of the primary set piece was quite clever, even brilliant, and key to almost every scene of the play. The night before our opening performance, construction on the giant shoe was still unfinished, much less painted. The props were incomplete, set doors hadn't been hung and our young actors had to run through their final dress rehearsal without the use of many of the set pieces they needed. The volunteer paint crew worked long into the night and arrived early the next day. When the curtains opened for the afternoon matinee, we were backstage praying the paint had dried and the performers would be able to successfully navigate their way around the stage. Fortunately, children are resilient and flexible; things worked out and the play was a great success.

Over the course of my many years with this theater group, this same scenario played out with artists and designers in every area of production. There were times we found set designers, music directors and choreographers that were able to communicate their vision and successfully lead their production teams. Others made it a more challenging experience, frustrating our young performers and leaving volunteers without the necessary information or tools. Some brought strong personal skills to their work and inspired and led their teams effectively, making it an enjoyable experience even with long hours of hard work.

There were times the pendulum swung the other direction. Occasionally, producers hired staff giving little thought to the artistry needed. They didn't understand or consider the artistic design needs of the production, and the aesthetic value suffered. Our most successful shows, and there have been many, effectively combined the highest level of artistry available to us, with strong organization and production skills. It was the talent and vision of the right-brain visual-spatials, combined with strong communication and sequencing skills of our auditory-sequentials. The entire company, even our young performers, felt more confident and enthused in those shows that combined with top-notch artistry, met deadlines, great production staff and effective communication.

## Right Needs Left

Art cannot be seen or shared if it stays in one's imagination. As artists, we must be able to manifest and communicate what we can imagine. Not all artists or designers are responsible for communicating with the production staff that implements their designs, but when they do, it will be necessary to communicate and structure what needs to happen to bring their designs to life. This is true of any artist. This was true of our costume and lighting designers, the music director, dance instructors and drama teachers.

Each of these right-brain, visual-spatial dominant artists came to the job with a vision for their part of the production and had to communicate their vision to other members of the team, to the individuals in charge and to the audience. To be successful, they needed to be good at more than their technical skills and creative skills. They need those auditory-sequential skills of the left-brain hemisphere, the attention to detail, logic, order, structure and the ability to communicate through spoken and written language, to do what needed to be done.

There are real life consequences to a lack of organizational ability. I was once told, "visionaries need implementers," and while I have seen and personally experienced this in my own workplace, I also know visionaries need their own implementation skills. While we may have strength in one or the other, it's just not enough to be one *without* the other. Visionary leaders need people with strong implementation skills to bring concepts to life. But as right-brain visual-spatials, the ability to implement what we envision and communicate effectively is critical to us as individuals.

Linda Silverman shares, "The right hemisphere is perceptive, receptive, and accepting, but it's incapable of action. It **is** rather than does. Is-ness is nice in the ethereal sense, but it doesn't feed your family. If you only exist and you don't do anything, what are you contributing? If you're totally work oriented, and never stop to smell the roses, where is the joy in living? You need both **being** and **doing** to be whole."[46]

As we embrace and develop visual-spatial abilities, we must also be diligent about developing our language and sequencing abilities. As we adapt education to speak visual-spatial language, we must also find ways to aid in the development of logic and sequencing skills. This kind of preparation is what is going to enable us to share and *do* all that our visual minds know we can *be*.

## Real Life Consequences

In my business, we recently worked on two software development projects, with two different developers, simultaneously. This experience allowed me to see the vast differences in working style and the way it affected the overall success of the project and the quality of life for those involved.

One programmer is a very left-brain individual, who worked with a right-brain project manager. The project manager had strong conceptual, relational and communication skills. He also had a high regard for structure, process and the use of organizational tools, which worked well for the left-brain programmer. The project manager and programmer communicated well with us, throughout the process, and used a detailed, written project plan to track activity and record change orders. This organization and documentation kept the project on track, enabled us to meet deadlines and saved everyone time and money.

Our second developer was extremely challenging and enormously delayed completing the project. He's a brilliant programmer, who's very committed to the project and servicing the end users. But he is also a right-brain visual-spatial who lacks some organizational skills. While the initial project needs were clearly defined, communicated and understood, poor planning on his part caused early delays in the project. Challenges snowballed from there. This developer didn't have project management tools in place and was not able to manage change orders effectively. Our internal team member tracked all communications, gathered feedback from testers, prioritized needs and communicated needed changes. But the developer was so scattered and unable to keep himself on track, that when asked to complete the top five items on the list, he worked on #7, #2 and #9. He even wandered off the list and worked on new features that were helpful, but not in the project plan. He had passion and a lot of great ideas, but couldn't deliver a finished product. His difficulty with focus, process and organization frustrated everyone involved and caused significant and costly delays.

# Lost Career

As a young child, I loved making things and doing art. I loved to color and was one of those kids that colored perfectly. I was so careful, so detailed and never went out of the lines. But when I went to elementary school and had to draw, I was really frustrated. I remember being in class and the teacher expecting us to draw, but don't remember her telling us how. I didn't know how to draw things the way I could see them, so I gave up.

My grandmother taught me needlepoint, and I was an excellent seamstress at an early age, making all my own clothes. I wanted to be an interior designer, so I enrolled in college with that as my major. After a few classes, my earlier drawing frustration was back, hindering my ability to complete the course work. The instructor was kind, and told me I had a good eye for design, but I still couldn't draw out the assignments. After a few classes, I decided to give up and switched from interior design to a major in textiles and clothing. Draping class was problematic when it came to drawing out my designs, but I managed to get through that one class to complete my degree. I minored in art history, because it was one way to be involved in art without having to draw!

As an adult, I still participate in a variety of art forms — sewing, cross stitch, quilting and decorating. I never became an interior designer, the career I really wanted, because I couldn't draw. Now, if I have to draw something it's still a painful experience. There are too many memories of wanting to do something so much and never learning how.

- Cindy Funk
*Manager of Finance & Reporting,*
*Young Rembrandts*

# 3

# Artists Want
# to Know

3

66 Others have seen what is and asked why.
I have seen what could be and asked why not. 99
- Pablo Picasso[47]

**A**S AN ART KID, I DID ART BECAUSE IT MADE ME HAPPY. As a right-brain thinker, I needed art. I now see how being adept in the world of creating, seeing and making images has been a significant aid to my thinking and learning process. Yet, as much as I loved art and art classes, it has always been accompanied by some degree of frustration and disappointment. Even as an adult, I have found it difficult to find the type of instruction that provided the training and techniques I wanted to learn.

There is a common perception in art that in order to protect a student's creativity, art needs to be taught without too much direct instruction. As a result, many art classes are focused on experiencing a variety of media, and while these experiences have significant value, there are enormous developmental opportunities being missed. As an art kid, I longed for detailed instruction, demonstration and information about how to draw what my visual mind could imagine. I wasn't worried about my creativity. I had plenty of that. What I wanted was the "how to" instruction I needed in order to share what I could imagine.

With literacy calling for a whole new level of visual and verbal capability, we have a tremendous opportunity to reconsider the way we teach art. By teaching art with more structure, demonstration and technical instruction, we can empower our visual and auditory learners with the tools they need to read, write, discern and think visually. This will benefit them as learners, but will also provide us the opportunity to transform the impact and perceived value of art education. By doing this, we don't lessen the value of art as creative expression. We strengthen it, by helping our students develop confidence, skill and a comprehensive art literacy.

## Elementary Art

In elementary school, I was one of the few art kids in the classroom. I attended a new elementary school every two years, because my dad's work transferred us. No matter where we went, there always seemed to be *just two* art kids in every class. We were well-respected by our classmates, the kids that won every art contest and led creative adventures.

At a young age, I was happy with anything I put on paper. The older I got, however, the more aware I became of the disparity between what I could see and what I could draw. Being visual, I had a heightened sense of observation. As a kid driven by shape, line and form, I had to draw. I had to do art. As a visual and artistic being, it gave life and breath to my soul. So even when my work failed to meet my expectations, I still spent endless hours on my own doing art. Though I was heralded as the artistic one, what was on paper was nothing close to what I intended. Every once in a while, I stumbled on a fresh insight or revelation about placing a shape or line to more accurately represent the image I was drawing. But as much as I loved and needed art, the process of doing and learning was a slow and steady stumble down a dark alley filled with self-doubt and discouragement.

Hungry to learn, I sometimes drew from library books. Audubon books, full of detailed bird drawings, were my favorite. I spent hours carefully copying the illustrations so I could learn how to draw birds and the details of their feathers and habitat. While my masterful drawings were admired for their realism, they were also perceived in a negative light because, in my day, you were not supposed to "copy."

## High School Art

Art in my elementary years had been a solo activity without ways to share the experience. I couldn't join a team or have the social outlet that sports or other clubs provided. But, in middle school, there were more art classes and new opportunities to be creative beyond the classroom. By high school, being artistic opened new doors, and I really started to come into my own. I became involved in everything from designing and building homecoming floats, painting school windows for special events, to set and costume design for theater productions. I was even asked to lead the committee that selected our class ring, because they thought I would "have good taste." As much as I enjoyed school and did well in all my classes, participation in after-school activities enriched my educational experience, engaged me socially and enabled multiple aspects of my personality and skills to develop.

High school art classes were not what I expected. The art department was considered one of the best in the area, and I took as many art classes as my schedule allowed. There was free choice in our classrooms and as long as we were being productive, we could explore any art form or subject matter. Our teacher checked on us regularly, and we were required to submit completed works, yet it never felt right. The room was full of art kids now, all of us doing our own thing, but there was no direction or real expectation. We were creating whatever we wanted, and yet it was very unsatisfying. It should have been a time to really grow in my artistic abilities and learn the techniques I longed for, but it wasn't. Instead, I continued the slow stumble down a dark alley filled with self-doubt and discouragement.

As a sophomore in high school, I was excited to be taking a real painting class. The instructor gave us our assignment; we thought about what we wanted to paint and then presented our ideas to him. He listened, gave some suggestions and sent us to our individual canvases to paint. The limited instruction was focused on how to use the paint, handle the brushes and clean up. There was no instruction on how to plan our composition, no thumbnail sketches, no information on mixing or using paint, how to plan and use color, or create volume and texture. So, as frustrated as I had been as an art kid drawing and sketching, it was then magnified by the addition of this new media.

> " *The more art classes I took, the more media I experienced, the more I felt lacking in my own abilities.* "

I was excited to be painting, but had no idea what I was doing. I wasn't happy with the actual drawing I was attempting to paint and didn't know how to make it better. We never discussed lighting, shading or realism verses abstraction. Instead of doing "real" art, I was plagued with more uncertainty and dissatisfaction. And since no one was talking about any of the things I felt so unsure about, I assumed we were just supposed to know. After all, we were the art kids. *But I didn't know*, and my paintings reflected that. The more I painted my bad drawings, the worse it all seemed to get.

I was graded on my effort, the time I put into the project and the way I applied the paint. Valiant attempts consistently met with good grades. And while I was thankful for good grades, they didn't reflect my feelings about the quality of my work. The more art classes I took, the more media I experienced, the more I felt lacking in my own abilities. I could see what I wanted to do. I was visual, discerning and could imagine so much more, so much better. However, there was never the conversation, demonstration or instruction on how to achieve what I could see.

By senior year, art classes were more of the same, but with a slightly different twist. Now there were more options. We could choose to paint, draw, sculpt or do photography. The teacher asked us how we wanted to express ourselves. Feeling unsuccessful after my painting experience, I stuck with drawing. Throughout both semesters senior year, there was a full room of art kids doing whatever kind of art we wanted. We sat on our stools and worked at our big art tables, each doing our own thing, some chatter and socializing happening while we "created". Every so often, we had class critiques where we discussed the art we were producing. Those were painful and unsatisfying experiences, not because of what might be said about our work, but because we didn't know what we were doing, or why, and had absolutely no idea how to talk about it.

While I was busy drawing the same old things I usually drew, I remember being envious of the students that chose to pursue photography. The instructor seemed to spend more time with them. There was lots of talk about how to use the camera and loads of instruction on the darkroom process. In that part of the classroom, there was always a good buzz in the air. It was the sound of discovery, new information, and new experiences. I was jealous, but didn't understand why.

## Expanding My Horizons

One of the most profound artistic experiences in my high school years happened when I became friends with Robin. We met in band. Yes, I was a "band nerd" as well as an "art nerd". She played the tuba and I played bassoon, not because of my stunning musical abilities, but because I had long fingers and the band needed a bassoonist. Robin's family was very different from mine. Her parents were well-educated and interested in the arts. As a family, they enjoyed evenings at orchestral hall and regular visits to art museums. My friendship with Robin and time with her family brought me fresh opportunities and revelations.

I stepped into a whole new world on my first visit to their family home. It was a modest suburban home, but everything in it was artistic in its design and choice. The focal point of the living room was a Chagall-style stain glass window. I had never seen anything like its intense colors and abstract design. Typical armchairs had been replaced by antique wooden benches. Beautifully designed vases, unique paintings, and decorative elements adorned their home. It was what I imagined an art museum to be.

I was invited to join family outings, and our trips to the Art Institute of Chicago opened wide a new world for me. We lived in a nearby suburb, only 45 minutes away, but I had never been there. I am still moved by the memory and emotion of those first experiences. It refreshed my soul after a young life of feeling parched. My visual nature longed for such an occasion,  for such feeding. I was stirred by every canvas, every encounter with a painting created so long ago. I felt a connection with the artists, how they saw the world, what they shared. It touched the deepest part of my soul. It fed me, encouraged me and brought me such utter and complete joy. It even touched that part of me that had started to doubt myself, my art. While those artists were infinitely superior, I could see their progression of experience and the evolution of their work. I started to understand gaining skill was a process and if I hung in there, maybe I could progress. Then perhaps I, too, could share the way I saw the world.

In high school, I was also blessed with a special group of friends who loved music, art and theater. Together, we made regular trips to the city, to the parks, to the art museum. Seeing our favorite paintings was like visiting old friends. We returned to the museum time after time to make "friends" with new styles of art. Attending art museums is still a favorite activity for me, and I'm especially fond of special exhibitions with audio tours, because it includes background information on the artists and the influences of their time. Seeing and experiencing art continues to feed my visual hunger, fuel my creativity and stir my soul.

## What Did I Learn?

After four years of high school art, math, English and science, I graduated without being taught the fundamentals of art. I never drew a still life. Never did observational drawing. Never learned to draw realistically. Never learned to use light and shadows to create volume. I never learned about art pencils or good drawing paper. I was given plenty of paint, but never learned how to paint or how to draw what I wanted to paint.

I was thankful for my exposure to master artists and art history, but it had come through friends and personal experiences. For me, elementary and high school art education had been open-ended exploration using a variety of media. We were free to create, but with little direction, demonstration and information. I worked hard, always striving to do my best, but always felt something lacking. And since every art class had been essentially the same in theory and practice, if something was lacking, again I assumed it must be me.

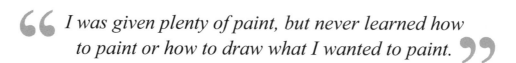

*I was given plenty of paint, but never learned how to paint or how to draw what I wanted to paint.*

I assumed that even though I loved art, loved to do art, I must not be that good at it. I was one of the art kids, but somehow didn't know enough of what I was supposed to know. I was born with some talent, but maybe not enough. But oddly enough, even with the dissatisfaction and self-doubt, art was still what I craved, what fed me, what I had to pursue.

## College Art

One of the key factors in my choice of college was driven by the reputation of its art department. I was sure this was where the "real" art instruction would come. I thought that being an art major, being immersed and devoted while enrolled in a strong program, would bring the satisfaction, tools and training I longed for. As a studio art major, I was blessed with a wide range of artistic experiences, from graphic design classes, drawing, figure drawing, watercolors, photography, weaving and lithography. But in time, I realized I wasn't getting as much demonstration and "how to" information as I had hoped. It didn't take long to see the same teaching philosophy I experienced earlier had followed me to college.

## "Real" Drawing Classes

All throughout college, I took drawing classes. Drawing was my passion, and success in drawing was foundational to success in other media. But sadly, drawing classes weren't always about drawing. Freshman drawing was taught by a teacher's assistant, who spent most of the semester trying to get us to broaden our understanding of what he thought constituted real art. Most of our class time was spent talking about art. Every week, we viewed slides of different styles of art and art forms. The instructor was especially fond of conceptual art, and we viewed examples of wrapped buildings and holes in the ground. In his class, we learned that realistic barn scenes were not art. Holes in the ground were.

My sophomore year drawing professor was a brilliant draftsman. I admired his drawings and was excited to study under him. While we didn't receive any direct demonstration or instruction, it was a valuable class. This instructor gave assignments designed for purposeful discovery. We learned to use numbered drawing pencils, high quality papers and gained an understanding of line and value. He also gave assignments that required us to use art to convey concepts. This is where my visual, spatial and conceptual thinking skills served me well, and when I realized they had value.

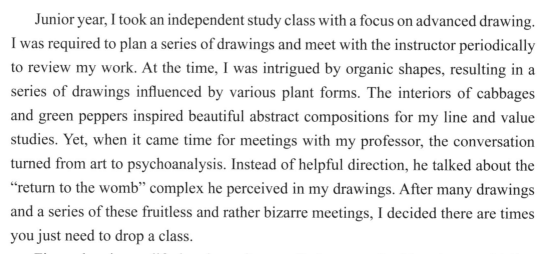

*After many drawings and a series of these fruitless
and rather bizarre meetings,
I decided there are times you just need to drop a class.*

Junior year, I took an independent study class with a focus on advanced drawing. I was required to plan a series of drawings and meet with the instructor periodically to review my work. At the time, I was intrigued by organic shapes, resulting in a series of drawings influenced by various plant forms. The interiors of cabbages and green peppers inspired beautiful abstract compositions for my line and value studies. Yet, when it came time for meetings with my professor, the conversation turned from art to psychoanalysis. Instead of helpful direction, he talked about the "return to the womb" complex he perceived in my drawings. After many drawings and a series of these fruitless and rather bizarre meetings, I decided there are times you just need to drop a class.

Figure drawing, or life drawing as it was called, was a refreshing change with live models. Every class period, we did quick study gesture drawings along with detailed observational drawings. We studied anatomy, proportion, scale and relationships. For homework, we were required to draw studies of hands, eyes, noses and other facial features. This class required us to draw from Albrecht Durer books and then create notebooks full of our own detailed observational studies. "Copying" was validated and even encouraged as a way to learn, and rightly so. Those pages and pages of eyes, ears, noses and hands did teach me to see, to observe. It trained me visually. The closer I looked, the better chance I had at drawing it realistically. The more I understood anatomy, the better I could represent it.

## Media

In weaving class, we learned about our yarns, the warp and weft, shuttles and the technical aspects of using floor looms. Photography class required a thorough understanding of camera mechanics and darkroom techniques. In lithography class, we spent endless hours preparing stones and learning the technical aspects of the printing process. All of these classes required equipment training, but didn't address the actual art we were producing.

My college watercolor class was an enormous disappointment. It was the same slow stumble down a dark alley of my youth, but this time with an instructor and his newspaper. Watercolors require a reasonable amount of technical skill and special ways to prepare the paper and handle the medium. After lugging heavy boards, paper and painting supplies across campus, I settled into class, excited and expecting demonstration on my new craft. The classroom contained large water trays for soaking paper and samples of leftover work with beautiful washes and unique textures. The teacher entered the room, introduced himself, shared his expectations for the semester and set us to work on our first assignment. Then he walked to the corner of the room and pulled out his newspaper. And that was our semester. He read the newspaper while we sat on our stools, at our big art tables and tried to figure out how to use watercolors. There were no demonstrations on how to prepare our paper, how to create those beautiful washes or unique textures. Nothing. We had assignments, grades and class critiques, all based on what we managed to figure out on our own.

Design class was a bit of reverse in teaching style. It was also one of the only times I remember an instructor pulling me aside for encouragement. It was basic two-dimensional design and we actually learned basic design fundamentals. I was delighted. We talked about elements of composition, and the assignments required us to demonstrate those principals. I

was finally learning foundational art and design concepts. But when it came to learning our tools, there was no instruction. It was expected that through practice and repetition we would gain the needed technical competency. That led to endless hours of hit and miss performance.

> 66 *Feelings of intense frustration, disappointment and loss washed over me. I could really be good at this, I knew I could. But I wanted more.* 99

Halfway through the semester, the instructor talked to me after class. He said, "You really have a gift. You have an innate sense of composition and design." I was surprised and flattered at the same time. It was the first time I could name something in art I was good at. It was also obvious my natural ability had been further developed because of the training I received in his class. This training, along with his encouragement, was very special to me and helped build some lost confidence. Maybe I could do this art thing after all. Maybe I did have some artistic ability. His class was strict, he had high expectations and was a tough grader, but he gave us the information we needed to be successful. I was disappointed when that instructor left the college the following year.

## Demonstration

On rare occasions, there were demonstrations in my media-based classes. First, the instructor talked about doing art. He talked and talked and talked about doing. Eventually, he started doing, and a room full of ready and willing students watched as a series of masterful strokes, lines and color filled his page. Then it was our turn. Tools in hand, we approached our paper and struggled to remember what he did. He encouraged us to jump in, go at it, explore the medium and see what it can do. But we were back at the beginning, not sure where to start, what to do, wanting to be successful and not knowing how. Feelings of intense frustration, disappointment and loss washed over me. I could really be good at this, I knew I could. But I wanted more.

What exactly did I want? I wanted someone to show me and let me follow them, step by step. I wanted to copy each stroke, each line, each application of color. I wanted to follow along a few times with this new medium just to gain a basic understanding. I wasn't worried about being creative. I knew that once I developed some basic competency, I could move on. I would be free to do my own work and create strokes, lines and colors that were my own. That's how the masters learned. That's how we learn music, math and science. I didn't understand why art class couldn't be the same.

## Slight Change of Direction

My dissatisfaction and general uncertainty about what to pursue in the arts led me to change schools and areas of focus. Obtaining my college degree was a lengthy process, involving more than one major and an overabundance of credit hours. After years spent working towards my studio arts degree, I transferred to a school that offered a fashion design and illustration program. I always had an interest in fashion and had learned to sew at a young age, creating collections of stylish Barbie clothes. Sewing was another creative outlet for me, and in high school, I made many of my own clothes along with costumes for theater productions. I thought fashion illustration might be an employable endeavor for my design and drawing skills, but was sadly disappointed in the illustration portion of the curriculum. We received excellent instruction in clothing construction and pattern making, but when it came to illustration and textile design, I experienced many of the same art education frustrations.

Fashion illustration classes were assignments without "how to" information. My earlier figure drawing classes gave me a distinct advantage over other students, because I had seen and studied the human figure underneath the fashionable clothes. My two-dimensional design class had prepared me for textile design, but we received no training on designing specifically for textiles. As porous as my own art training had been, the majority of students in this program had no previous art training. These new college students were thrown into these illustration and design classes without training in art fundamentals, figure drawing or principles of design.

After two years in this program, I graduated with a degree in fashion design and construction. With a lot of hard work and a healthy dose of frustration, I had become a good designer, an excellent seamstress and was able to draft my own patterns. I had learned to take a project from inception to completion through concept, design, construction and presentation. I participated in fashion shows and even sold a few designs to a local dress manufacturer, but still didn't know enough about illustration to pursue the career that originally brought me to the school.

## Graduation

Eventually, I went back to my original college and completed my advanced art classes while working full time. I graduated *Magna Cum Laud* with a Bachelor of Fine Arts. But overall, art education in college had been an open-ended exploration using a variety of media. As art students, we created whatever we wanted to create without training in basic technical skills. For the most part, training demonstration and "how to" instruction had been reserved for mechanical applications, using cameras, looms and printing stones. Once again, I was left feeling that art majors were just supposed to know things. And since I didn't *just*

*know*, even with an art degree, perhaps I wasn't meant to do art. There were so many holes in my education, so many things I never learned.

Mine was not a unique experience. This method of teaching art experientially is very common in schools and universities. Many of the professional artists I have encountered have been self-taught, even those with college degrees. There is a fortunate minority that attended schools that understood the need to train students in the technical skills of art, much like master artists were trained. They were taught the elements, principles and "rules" of art. They could be creative, because they could choose to maintain the rules or break the rules. Once they had skills mastered, and knew what the rules were, these artists were free to express what they wanted to express.

We are doing high school and college art students an enormous disservice by graduating them without developing their visual and communication skills, and also not preparing those that do want to move on to professional art careers. I recently met an administrator of an animation college in Canada, the Sheridan Institute of Technology, dubbed the "Harvard of animation school" by animator Michael Hirsch in 1996. The administrator I spoke with commented on the entrance requirements for incoming animation students and the rigorous portfolio requirements, stating, "The Sheridan Institute of Technology receives over 1100 applications into our Bachelor of Applied Arts in Animation annually, for 110 seats. Students have to submit a rigorous portfolio showcasing their knowledge of structure, line drawing, character movement, story boarding, expressions and still life."

If applying students haven't been prepared to enter the program, they have the opportunity to attend a preliminary program that teaches them the fundamentals of art. "Students who do not gain entry into our animation program can enroll in our Arts Fundamentals one year certificate program where they learn the basic skills in line and life drawing to build a portfolio for submission into the animation program during subsequent intake years."[48] But why should these students have to spend time and money to attend a special program that teaches them the basic line and life drawing skills they should have already learned?

There are students everywhere not being trained in the fundamentals they need to move on to more advanced study. And the ones that still want to try may not be fortunate enough to get into such a program or find this kind of training. We risk lost careers and undeveloped talent by not preparing our students. This would be considered a travesty in math, science and other left-brain areas of study. It's just as much a travesty in the visual arts.

## Time to Get a Job

After years of education and tons of creative experiences, but few real skills developed in the arts, it was time to get a job. I was fortunate to find a job at a small graphic arts firm that specialized in point of purchase displays. It was my first time working in an art-related business and I was ready to learn. I wasn't hired to do art. I was hired as an assistant to the owner. He met with clients, came back to the office, debriefed us, and I helped organize the tasks that needed to be completed. As much as I am artistic, creative, conceptual and big picture, I also have strong administrative skills. This was a good fit for both my art and organizing abilities.

Surprisingly to me, my art education continued as I worked alongside professional graphic artists and freelance illustrators. I was enormously appreciative of every new trick or technique I learned, but consistently wondered why I hadn't

learned them as an art student. One day, I came across a mock-up of a very large display for one of our grocery store accounts. In my day, B.C. (before computers), designs and mock ups were drawn and colored by hand, requiring masterful technique by the artist. This particular mock-up had very large areas requiring colored marker, and it had been applied impeccably. Later that day, the artist demonstrated his technique for me. Using a very long ruler to guide his marker, he applied long, straight, evenly spaced lines of color. He continued to add rows of carefully placed color until the entire area was complete. The process required patience and a calm, steady hand, but was simple and easy to do.

Working with professional illustrators revealed things that empowered me and restored more of my lost artistic confidence. I had often struggled drawing something not completely familiar to me. When teachers said, "Draw a jungle animal," then focused the instruction on the painting process, I assumed we were just supposed to know how to draw the jungle animals. After all, that was part of being an art kid. People seemed to think if we had some natural talent, we could draw anything. I did have innate ability, but there was plenty I didn't know.

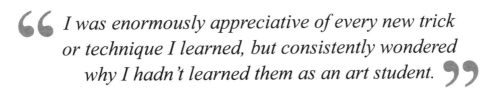

*I was enormously appreciative of every new trick or technique I learned, but consistently wondered why I hadn't learned them as an art student.*

These professionals also exposed the big "secret" — *they used reference material!* Artists kept files and files of images, so when they needed to draw something they could look it up. Remember, these were the days before computers and the internet. These artists preferred to draw from life, but if that wasn't available, they had files and files of pictures to reference. So while "copying" wasn't the goal, looking at resources was enormously helpful to learning more about the subject matter.

This was real news to me. It was also permission. To draw effectively, we need to look at what we want to draw. We need to see it, study the details, unique features and subtle nuances. Details and important features are key to realistic drawing and can be a component of abstraction. Once we know it, we can draw it, interpret it, even design or abstract it. Now all of this seems pretty obvious, but knowing it sooner, knowing it in school, would have been helpful.

## The Business of Art

Eventually, I moved from project management to the agency's art department. I learned to spec and print type, assist on photo shoots, do design and layout work. My time in a professional design house also gave me insights on the business of art, working to deadlines, meeting and exceeding customers' expectations and being creative while designing to the clients' specifications. As artists, we had to be fiscally responsible. There weren't endless payroll hours to create. There were guidelines, timelines and assignments, and we were expected to produce work of the highest artistic caliber within those parameters. There wasn't time to stop and learn technique or art fundamentals while on the job. Art professionals are expected to come to the job with foundational proficiency. They work to develop higher levels of artistry and creativity, while being consistent, timely and professional in their delivery.

My work in design and illustration helped me develop additional skills, but I clearly had not come prepared with the same level of technical skill they had. So when it was time to move to my next job, I pursued other types of work, often not art related. Many of us art kids give up, change majors or change careers. I worked in retail management, was a buyer for a clothing store and even did a brief stint at a local bank before I found my way back to art.

Eventually, I gained some proficiency with watercolors, my favorite media next to drawing and color pencil. But most of what I learned came through technique books and trial and error. Once I was married and had children, I worked as an artist, painting watercolor portraits of children, before I started teaching others the art techniques I had so longed to know.

## Art Literacy

Overall, the lack of technical training in art education limited what I have been able to create. I didn't build the depth of skill and mastery of media required to freely create what I could so easily imagine. There have been numerous times over the years that a scene or idea captivated me, and I longed to share it. As the creative juices flowed, I delighted in planning the composition, colors and media I would use. But often I came to an abrupt stop when I realized what would have to be learned in order to paint what I could see. I could draw and create a strong composition, but I would need to teach myself specific techniques in order to paint it.

I couldn't find classes that taught the demonstration and "how to" technique, but knew I would find helpful books. I thought about the time it would take to find the information, learn the needed skills and attain a level of proficiency.

> *Doing art without a strong foundation in technique and media mastery is like starting over every time. It becomes exhausting, discouraging and robs us of our creative power.*

But when I compared all that needed to happen against the one painting I wanted to complete, I grew discouraged. It was like finding a great book to read, but realizing you need to learn a whole new language before you *can* read it. Doing art without a strong foundation in technique and media mastery is like starting over every time. It becomes exhausting, discouraging and robs us of our creative power.

Mine is not an unusual situation. There are limitless numbers of paintings never completed, artistic visions never birthed or given form, all because of a lack of tools, training and understanding. Sadly, we think the problem lies in us, art kids and non-art kids. We think we are just supposed to know how to draw, how to do

**3**

art. But it's not about us, it never was. It wasn't because we didn't know enough. It was the style of teaching that was not sufficient. Even if we were born with some innate artistic ability, it's quite unreasonable to think we were also born with a complete understanding and proficiency.

## Technical Training

Technical training that includes learning to draw gives children tools in their tool belt. Drawing is the foundation of the visual arts. To paint a picture, we first have to draw the picture. To use pastels, paints and other art media successfully, requires a strong foundation in drawing and the elements of art. One must also know the "rules" of art to do art. The master artists, Rembrandt, Vermeer and Degas, were technically trained. At a relatively young age, they entered formal apprentice programs where they learned the basic principles of art: line, form, composition, volume, light, shadow and color. They worked under professional artists and craftsmen applying and honing their skills. Once they mastered their craft, they worked independently as artists, creating their own works of art. They used their well-developed skills to record and interpret the world around them, communicating and expressing with their unique voice. But first came the technical training.

One of the delights of studying art history and individual artists is seeing the transformation of an individual artist's style over the course of their careers. In the early years, artists show a formality and reasonableness to their work, a connection to the art of their day. It's as if their technical training rules their communications. As the artist gains mastery, independent opinion, interpretation and thought, their work represents their growing individuality.

When did art education become less about skill training and more about expression and experience? For me, it seems to parallel the decline of realism in art and the rise of abstract art and expressionism. Early man, like young children, used art to document events and share stories. Over the centuries, as mankind and materials evolved, art became increasingly realistic and sophisticated, as evidenced by Greco Roman art, the Renaissance and Neoclassicism. Artists were finely trained craftsmen with incredible mastery of their tools, taking great pride in their ability to create increasingly realistic images of the world around them.

In the late 19th century, Impressionists broke away from the tradition of realism, using light and dashes of color to represent form. Yet these artists were formally trained and able to create realistic works of art, but they *chose* to interpret the world more abstractly. There were a series of art movements in the early 20th century that challenged traditional views of art, moving heavily into abstract images and experiential art. The *fauves* focused on the use of bold colors to convey feelings. The cubists were concerned with dimension and spatial planes; the abstract expressionists championed the elements of art over subject matter.

Pablo Picasso (1881-1973) is well known for his abstract art and its profound impact on the 20th century art movement. Yet Picasso's early training and mastery of realism is often unknown and overlooked. Picasso was trained

Pablo Picasso. First Communion. (1895-96). *Painted at 14 years old.*
© 2010 Estate of Pablo Picasso / Artists Rights Society (ARS), New York

BEING VISUAL

Pablo Picasso. Nude and Still Life. (1931). © 2010 Estate of Pablo Picasso / Artists Rights Society (ARS), New York

by his father, an artist, museum curator and art instructor, who often allowed him to finish details in his own paintings.

Pablo's ability to replicate and paint realistically in his early teen years was extraordinary. Having mastered realism at an early age, he looked for new challenges, new ways to see and express himself. It's as if he said, *I can paint it as I see it, so now what else?* He spent the rest of his impressive career exploring various components of art, line, form, color and dimension, creating a tremendous volume of powerful and influential work.

Picasso's pursuit of new realms of possibility was representative of the modern art movement's quest for new frontiers and new visual experiences. Abstract artists intentionally turned away from representational images. Artists like Mark Rothko (1903-1970), Jackson Pollock (1912-1956), and Frank Stella (1936- ) are held in high regard. Their contribution and artistic expression is valued, but much of the general population still wonders why their drips of paint, geometric shapes or blocks of color are considered art. They don't understand why a solid black canvas painted by Rothko is any different than a canvas anyone could paint black. And if this black canvas is art, then why would we need to train anyone to do art? It doesn't seem to require any specific skill. Just

Pablo Picasso. The Sailor. (1938). © 2010 Estate of Pablo Picasso / Artists Rights Society (ARS), New York

put a child in front of that easel with a jar of paint and let them create like these modern artists seemed to paint — loose, abstract and anything goes. But not all black canvases are the same.

Pablo Picasso. Petite Fleurs. (1958).
© 2010 Estate of Pablo Picasso / Artists Rights Society (ARS), New York

I contend that while abstract art is a reality, it has created a false sense of what art is or should be in relation to young children and creativity. Modern art's influence has drawn us away from seeing the need to train in the technical aspects of art. It has impacted art education theory and changed the way we train art students from pre-school to college, perpetuating the false assumption that art should be created without regard for its technical aspects. It implies that *true art* is spontaneous, unhindered expression. However, my own experience as a child, teen, college student and adult artist did not support that theory. I don't want to paint abstractly, just because I don't know any other way. I wanted foundational training; training that covered all the basic skills, so I could do what I wanted to do. So I could draw and paint what I want to paint. I wanted the ability to choose as earlier artists had; but without that training, the ability to express myself was greatly limited.

## Children Want Real

Children come to the easel wanting to say something, wanting to share themselves. They want to draw a picture of their mom, dad, family or house. They want to tell you who they are, show you who they are and have no interest in being abstract about it. They want *real* because they are working hard at this stage of life to *understand real*. Our young children want to communicate. They need the skills, mastery of their tools and training that allow them to draw and communicate what they want to say. We're all delighted when a four-year-old can draw a stick figure. But it's not so cute when they are fourteen, twenty-four or forty. Along with visual literacy skills, helping children develop technical skills provides a solid foundation in the visual arts and a means of communication. It also allows them to continue doing art long past the "crisis of confidence" stage. To deny them this type of training is to handicap them for life.

## Skill Requires Training

Art kids — all kids — have a predisposition to being visual, a desire to express themselves, and are drawn to make and see and do. But we all need information, training and systematic skill development to gain any level of competency. In all other forms of art, such as music, dance, theater and creative writing, there is a predetermined, systematic method of training. It is expected that with practice and repetition students will gain mastery of their craft and instrument that leads to freedom of expression and creativity.

> 66 *Art training requires the same structure, time, discipline and planned skill acquisition as math, science and reading.* 99

To learn music, one learns the grammar of music while training on a particular instrument. Dancers learn to dance with rigorous and skill-specific physical training. Writers write after being trained in letters, words, grammar and language usage. We cannot become proficient in the visual arts only by *experiencing* art. Students need codified, systematic training in the technical skills of the visual arts to become adept in producing and creating art. That means learning how to see, how to draw, how to use color, how to paint, shadow, texture and more.

Now consider the kids with less natural aptitude for drawing and art. When taught with the experiential, media-centered approach to art that is void of technical training, they have an even higher rate of discouragement and disappointment. This leaves them feeling unable or unqualified to participate in art. Without the innate drive that keeps art kids going until they find the information they need, these kids quit. They give up. They stop doing art and don't consider themselves capable. And somehow, this has become acceptable. There is an agreement in the education community that not everyone needs art, or is meant to do art, so not being proficient is excused. And yet we do not consider math, science, reading or writing optional. Regardless of a child's early or latent signs of natural ability in these subjects, we provide all school-age children with skill-specific training, knowing it is the information and training that develops their abilities.

All children, art kids and non-art kids, need training in the visual arts. With the majority of students relying on their visual skills to think and learn and literacy skills requiring visual mastery, this has become even more critical. Art is not for the select few, just as reading and writing are no longer for the elite. Everyone needs to develop their art and visual skills, to be successful as learners. Art training requires the same structure, time, discipline and planned skill acquisition as math, science and reading.

## Everyone's An Artist

I have often had the pleasure of going into an elementary classroom and teaching the whole class one of my "how to" draw lessons. One particular day, I tested my "art kid" theory on a room full of second graders. I walked into the room to find twenty-six smiling ready and willing faces. I introduced myself, saying I was there to teach them how to draw. With great excitement in the air, they cleared their desks. I asked "Who are the artists in this class?" The students proudly and unanimously pointed to the "art kids." There were two in this group of eight-year-old children. The art kids were happy to be recognized and nodded in agreement. Then, I asked the whole class to suspend judgment and not think of themselves as artists or non-artists and to be open minded as we did our drawing lesson together. I also assured them I would show them everything they needed to know to be able to complete the assignment.

For this particular class, I presented a "mature" kind of drawing lesson, an apple still life. In the drawing, an apple sat on a table with light shining, a shadow under it and a simple background behind. There would be no color in our drawing, since we would use only pencil to create values, shadows and reflected light. When the young

students first saw what we were going to draw, there was some hesitancy. But again, I assured them I would provide what they needed to be able to do this kind of work.

First, I placed a real apple on the table and turned off the classroom lights. My captive audience was very attentive and carefully watched as my flashlight demonstrated shadows and reflected light. Every eye watched as the position of the flashlight changed and the location of the shadows changed. With this visual, verbal and physical example of concept complete, we were ready to begin drawing. With paper and pencils distributed, I drew out the lesson, one step at a time. As I drew the apple on my paper, they watched and drew their apple. When I added the table line, they added the table line. We talked about the light source being on the upper right of the page which meant the table shadow would fall on the table, to the left of the apple. We all drew shadows. Next, we added shapes for the light reflected on our apple and the shadows on the body of the apple. Once each student added their background design, it was time to use pencil to complete our drawing.

The process of coloring in the apple and shadows was a step-by-step learning process. As I demonstrated, the students followed along doing the same to their drawings. We applied a medium grey value to the majority of our apple, a darker value to the shadow areas and left the reflected light area white. We put great attention on our pencil to maintain careful, steady strokes, turning the page as needed so we didn't lay our hands on top of our dark shadow areas full of pencil. As we moved through the lesson, I gave the exact same instruction to every student, without being mindful of who the "art kids" were. The students were attentive to the task at hand, all engaged and enjoying the activity. There was an age appropriate seriousness in the classroom, a sense of doing something very significant. Every student worked equally hard, and as the lesson progressed, the students went from uncertainty and doubt to a new-found confidence.

With the drawings complete, I mounted them on black construction paper and together as a class, we went into the hallway to hang them. The students stood patiently, as I carefully hung each drawing on the wall outside their classroom. As a group, we stepped back and viewed the collection of drawings. One by one came a smile of recognition as each student saw their drawing displayed. As I viewed the body of work, I noticed there was no clear differentiation of the "artists" and "non-artists." The playing field had been leveled. They all received demonstration and step-by-step instructions on how to draw, learned where shadows were in relation to light and how to apply pencil to create values and shades of gray. They were given the information they needed to be able to do the drawing. They all completed the drawing and shading lesson very successfully. They had all excelled.

# Opportunities to Create

In the summer and fall of 2011, our company, Michaels, decided to participate in Operation Christmas Cards. The organization's goal was to deliver 175,000 multinational holiday cards to our soldiers overseas. As a retail organization, we decided to actively facilitate the card making process by hosting Operation Christmas Card events. In early September, we participated in a neighborhood block party to make greeting cards for the troops at Wrigley Field, a well-known Chicago baseball park. One of our key vendors, EKSuccess Brands, donated and staffed the event and provided a generous assortment of art and craft supplies. Participants were provided a wonderful assortment of card stock, envelopes, stickers, archival pins, borders, colorful papers and markers. With plenty of publicity to spread the word, we encouraged people to come and create with us.

The event was open to anyone and everyone. All day long, men, women and children came streaming into the tent. Some would-be card makers were there to attend the game, others arrived fresh from tailgating or nearby restaurants. The response was overwhelming and the atmosphere warm and exciting. Strangers seemed friendlier in each other's presence, because they were there for a shared purpose and activity.

Creative crafters, and "non-creative" people alike, were united by the cause. The diversity of responses was amazing to see. Many people created their cards independently, others worked together. Some made very simple cards with stickers and brief words, but for others it was an in-depth process. There were even big, brawny manly men, straight from tailgate parties, making cards. They didn't seem the card making, crafting type, but in this purposeful, well-prepared, safe environment, they were motivated to do something creative.

What we saw at the Wrigley Field event was a microcosm of the overall effort. The number of cards made far surpassed our expectations, with over 315,000 cards collected and distributed by the organization. More than 50% of the hundreds of thousands of cards distributed went to soldiers that didn't receive any other cards or letters, so the holiday wishes felt especially impactful.

We firmly believe people want opportunities to create and craft. The organized card making events, activities in our retail stores and community response to the projects demonstrated this time and time again. The availability of materials, preparation and encouraging staff members made it easy for people to engage. Overall, they were less inhibited, enjoyed the activity and felt good about participating in a good cause.

- April Willers
*Director of Customer Experience,*
*Michaels Stores, Inc.*

# 4

# See, Touch, Do Learning

> " We discovered that education is not something which the teacher does, but that it is a natural process which develops spontaneously in the human being. It is not acquired by listening to words, but in virtue of experiences in which the child acts in his environment. "
>
> - Maria Montessori[49]

AFTER YEARS OF WORKING and my college degree in hand, my husband and I moved to a nearby Chicago suburb to start a family. We bought our first real house with room for kids and grass to mow. An extra bedroom held my drawing table, pencils and watercolors. While I continued to enjoy a variety of creative outlets, our first child, Laurie, was born, and my attention found a new focus. As a new mother I was eager to explore child development theories and learning styles. I read a variety of books that outlined the significant visual, physical, mental and muscular developments happening in my baby, and delighted in creating ways to facilitate my daughter's developments.

This curiosity led me to discover Montessori education and changed the course of my life. When we moved and started our family, our next-door neighbor, Deborah, owned two Montessori pre-schools. I had read about Montessori education in a college class and, even with minimal exposure, it intrigued me. Now as a mother, I was anxious to learn more and I had a living, breathing Montessori expert right next door. We became close friends, and Montessori philosophy and educational theory permeated our daily conversations. Eventually, I worked at both her schools, sent our kids to Montessori pre-schools and was profoundly affected by my involvement.

Montessori education is an educational philosophy that uses visual, tactile learning experiences to engage and educate, while being intentional about helping children develop internal discipline, order and structure. As a visual-spatial learner, with a tendency towards ADD behavior, this philosophy resonated with me. I needed multisensory experiences to learn, and their method of developing the structure and order that's so critical was effective, yet invisible to the child. It seemed the perfect combination.

One hundred years later, neuroscience has confirmed that multisensory learning is exactly what young children need as they build neural networks and dendrite forests. But multisensory learning doesn't end in pre-school. Educational theorists have identified a variety of sensory learning styles, which explains many of the challenges we face with an education system that is focused on the auditory-sequential learner. It turns out, there are many ways to assess intelligence and describe the other kinds of "smart" we are.

## Learning Montessori

Montessori education is based on the work of Maria Montessori, a woman ahead of her time, a pioneer. Maria was born in Italy in 1870 and the first woman to graduate from medical school at the University of Rome. She studied to be a pediatrician, later returning to volunteer at the university's psychology department. Maria became interested in educational theory and child development, and in 1900 was named the director of a school for mentally handicapped children in Rome. Her educational theories, which later became known as the Montessori Method, were initially influenced by earlier educational concepts, including those of Friedrich Frobel, who established the first kindergarten, and Jean Marc-Gaspard Itard, a

French physician and educator. Both Frobel and Itard emphasized the inherent potential of children and the need for an education system that recognized natural child development.

It turns out that while influenced by these earlier theories, Montessori consistently challenged educational theories based on the behavior and learning patterns she observed when working with children. She developed her own unique educational philosophy from clinical observations and scientific methods, and it proved to be successful with the mentally handicapped children under her instruction. When she saw the progress her students were making, she was convinced that applying similar methods to teaching "normal" children would develop their abilities as well.

> *Montessori education strives to 'discover the true nature of the child and then assist him in his normal development.'*

What intrigued me, right from the start, was the way Montessori education used engaging multisensory, every day activities to help children develop internal order and learning skills. The objective of Montessori education is to develop self-directed, self-motivated and self-regulated children with a lifelong love for learning. Montessori spoke often about discipline and ambition being internal and the need for children to be taught to listen to their inner motivators. Above all, she believed it was of utmost importance for children to develop internal order, internal discipline and their own internal call to action. While developing powerful cognitive abilities, Montessori children are also prepared for successful learning by developing critical processing capabilities: focus, order, patterning, time on task, discernment and completing cycles of activity.

Maria Montessori believed that within each child is the adult they will become. The role of the educator is to create opportunity, prepare materials and the environment while directing children in accordance with the rules of morality and society. Montessori education strives to "discover the true nature of the child and then assist him in his normal development." The philosophy is based on three important principles: observation, individual liberty and preparation of the environment. Close observation respects the inherent uniqueness of children and allows for self-determinism within a carefully prepared environment. Carefully prepared, self-connecting multisensory activities are key components of the prepared environment and allow for purposeful self-discovery and individual liberty.

Montessori was among the first to identify birth to six as years most critical to a child's development. This is when the "absorbent mind" naturally incorporates experiences into the child's basic character and personality for life. Montessori compared young minds to sponges, eagerly seeking out, decoding and mentally organizing the details of the world around them. Understanding the significance of these early years has since inspired many parents and educators to provide a wealth of meaningful experiences, so young minds will be suitably fed.

I was surprised to hear how popular Montessori education had been very early on and its conflict with the education community. By 1913, Montessori education had spread to more than 100 schools in the United States. Alexander Graham Bell and Thomas Edison were early supporters of the method. However, Montessori's philosophy was in direct conflict with turn of the century theories of "fixed intelligence" and objections to educating young children. Disputes with the professional teaching community limited its impact and many of the early schools disappeared. The method and its followers did continue to grow and flourish throughout Europe, with a resurgence here in America in the late 1950's.

Many elements of Montessori's philosophy have been incorporated into current teaching environments. Child-sized tables and chairs found in today's pre-schools and kindergartens are a direct result of Dr. Montessori's "preparation of the environment" principle. Modern day playground equipment was developed as a result of Montessori's observation of a child's need to move and develop gross motor skills. Individualized learning, readiness programs, math manipulatives and tactile learning tools have also become part of our current education system.

## The Classroom

Montessori education is first and foremost a philosophy. Montessori schools are independently owned, and application of the method can vary greatly. The Montessori method itself was and can still be misunderstood and misinterpreted, even today. Some critics feel the method is too rigid, while others claim it's too flexible for young children. For me, when I observed children busy "at work" in the Montessori classroom, it made sense. There was something remarkable, yet unexplained, going on. I saw many three to five-year-old children in the same classroom, all busy, involved and mesmerized by the activity in which they were involved. There was a strong sense of calm, order and respect, even with so many different activities and quiet conversations going on simultaneously. The children were engaged, self-directed, happy and on-task.

The classroom I observed was divided into several different areas: practical life, sensorial, math, science, language and gross motor play. Within each area were a variety of activities relative to the particular subject. The materials for each activity were self-contained in an attractive tray, box or basket, and placed on shelves where children were free to self-select. Without direction from the adult in the room, children went to a shelf, chose an activity and carried it to a small table or floor mat. When at a table or floor mat, they used the prepared materials as they worked through the particular activity. Once finished, the box or basket was refilled and carried back to its place on the shelf. The teacher, or directress as they are called in a Montessori classroom, moved quietly around the room overseeing, helping and redirecting as needed. This process of individual liberty within a prepared environment repeated itself all around the quiet classroom with children working independently, in pairs or in small groups.

The classroom materials were not what I expected to find. My only other exposure to groups of young children in a pre-school setting included brightly colored plastic toys strewn about the room. Montessori schools use a combination of teacher made materials and materials manufactured specifically for the Montessori

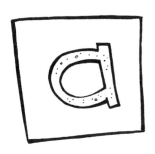

community. Montessori-designed materials are simple, yet enticing. All are designed for specific skill acquisition, such as understanding and experiencing gradients of size or volume, scale and numbers. This includes everything from red and blue rods to introduce beginning numeration, to sandpaper letters that initiate reading and language skills. There are a variety of engaging activities that use colorful beads and manipulatives to familiarize children with numbers, values and basic math concepts. The visual, tactile, colorful items invite young children to see, touch and interact. Through this multisensory play and self-discovery, and observing the behavior rules of the classroom, children gain self-mastery, initiative, self-confidence, learning skills and internal discipline.

One of my favorite parts of the Montessori classroom was the practical life area. It was filled with activities for children that mimic things found in their daily life — washing dishes, preparing snacks, pouring, sorting, dressing or buttoning. By mastering these

activities, children become skilled in life tasks, but, like all Montessori activities, these are also designed to entice and engage. The more engaging an activity, the longer the child will participate — resulting in extended time on task and "lost in the moment" experiences.

Montessori recognized the value of silence and was intentional about creating times for young children to experience quiet, enabling a deeper connection to self. When children spend time in quiet and contemplative thought, it allows them to hear their own thoughts, process information and organize new ideas. Being quiet enough to hear one's inner voice is critical to internal discipline, order learning and creativity.

Many activities in the Montessori classroom use visual, tactile exercises to help children learn to organize and sequence a series of steps. Hand washing is an example of a multi-step process. We may take it for granted, but Montessori uses this activity as a way for children to learn to order a complex series of steps. Kids are attracted to any type of water activity — add soap, bubbles and a nifty apron, and they are willing to do it again and again, making the learning feel more like fun than learning. The ability to order and sequence a series of steps, thoughts and actions is a critical life and learning skill, especially for our visual-spatial students, with less natural sequencing aptitude. Early mastery will enhance learning and brain function. Developing these critical skills while being involved in a fun, multisensory activity allows children to learn concepts in an effortless and spontaneous manner.

> ❝ *Many activities in the Montessori classroom use visual, tactile exercises to help children learn to organize and sequence a series of steps.* ❞

There are a variety of visual, tactile tools in the Montessori classroom, designed to engage and train the mind and senses. The colorful materials are specifically structured so children learn to arrange and pattern left to right, smallest to largest, narrow to wide. One of the most profound revelations I had was seeing the ways manipulatives and kinesthetic, tactile activities were used to teach math. My favorite tools were the "golden beads". Young children are tasked with learning the powers of ten, 1, 10, 100 and 1000, and they need to understand the name of the number they represent, the value and how they are related. But these numbers are very similar, visually, their slight visual differences out of scale with the difference in their values. This is challenging to grasp conceptually, so Montessori kids get to see, touch and feel 1, 10, 100 and 1000 by using prepared sets of golden beads. To gain understanding, they do numerous exercises with these beautiful tactile beads while pairing them with written symbols. When children hold a "1" bead in their right hand and a cube of "1000" beads in their left, their relative difference is seen, felt and understood at a deep cognitive level. It's a visual, kinesthetic experience. As they learn to assign written symbols to each set of beads, the relative number of zeros makes sense. This exercise uses multiple sensory experiences to gain a solid understanding of a subject.

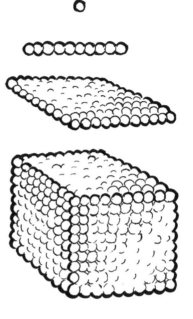

Fortunately, many elementary schools now have manipulatives as part of their math curriculum, giving students tactile experiences to help them grasp abstract concepts. Yet there are still limitless ways visual and sensory experiences can be used to enhance learning in math, science and other subject matter, especially as children mature and enter higher levels of education.

## Montessori At Home

Over a period of several years, I worked at both of my friends' Montessori schools. I loved pre-school students and continued to learn about child development from Montessori and a variety of other sources. While I studied skill development, language acquisition and best educational practices, I put the theories and best practices I studied into play at home. Our home was a structured, visual, prepared environment so the kids could operate independently at an early age. We had well-organized activities and tools ready for them to self-select, and I enjoyed creating ways to help them understand concepts and gain mastery of skills.

Our kitchen was organized with plates, cups and appropriate food items in lower cabinets, easily within a child's reach. I structured activities that involved doing, making and being, instead of the passive participation that television provided. A wealth of crafts and art materials were available as visual, kinesthetic and tactile ways to engage them. Legos, puzzles, blocks of wood, paint and glue were tools for three-dimensional creativity, developing their physical and spatial awareness. Building materials, dress-up clothes, props and imaginary play engaged all their senses, involving them for extended play times. Pencils, crayons and markers helped with fine motor development, observation and patterning skills.

With as many types of creative activities we made available, it was always done within the context of order and a prepared environment. Like the Montessori environment, costumes had to be hung up, props back on shelves and activities back in order. This assured that the value of participating in multisensory experiences also carried with it the potential to develop discipline, internal order, sequencing and organizational skills.

Our children attended Montessori school through kindergarten, and our home reinforced the learning they were experiencing. We felt this foundation of "learning to learn" skills prepared them for formal education and for their future as self-directed thinkers. Later, when we understood more about the needs of visual-spatial learners, we were thankful they had an early education experience that enabled them to learn visually, while developing the internal sense of order they so needed. Now, as adults, they still have fond memories of their home and classroom experiences and a great affection for Montessori materials.

## Grown Up Montessori

My participation in Montessori education taught me to become more aware of the way I operated on a day-to-day basis. This was enormously significant to me as a visual-spatial adult. I had always been easily distracted, moving from activity to activity, rarely finishing one thing before moving on to the next. My mind constantly raced, and while I liked order in the environment around me, I gained a clearer understanding of its affect on me. Being more aware of the goals and methods of the Montessori classroom helped me see areas I could manage better and, in the long run, allowed me to operate more successfully in life.

One day, while raking fall leaves, I saw a very clear demonstration of my deficiency in completing one cycle of activity before starting another. Sore armed from raking, I paused to review my progress. Instead of one large pile of leaves, my tendency towards distraction had manifested in 15 small leaf piles. In our neighborhood, disposing of leaves required a few large, strategically placed piles swept onto a large sheet of plastic and dragged to the front curb. My scattered and fragmented working style was strewn about the yard with no single pile of leaves ready for removal. I saw that I needed to apply the same philosophy of completing cycles of activity our preschoolers were learning to my own life.

I also noticed I have always been drawn to "practical life" activities, using them to disconnect and brew on ideas, returning later to find conclusions or move on to next steps. When working, creating art or writing, I often pause to let things settle a bit. Peeling potatoes, cutting apples or preparing the environment allows my hands to stay in motion while my mind processes, reviews and organizes a variety of thoughts. Understanding my needs as a visual learner, I became more intentional about allowing myself to use these types of activities to disconnect while my mind kept working.

I also realized my inherent need to create order and prepare the environment helped to clear and prepare my mind. I need to make my bed, tidy my room and be sure things are in their place before I get on with new activity each day. Turns out it wasn't a distraction or a bunny trail, it was actually quite helpful. When I organize the house for family members to be successful and independent, it creates the foundational structure my visual-spatials need. Coats, keys and shoes all have their place, workspaces are clearly designated and the kitchen is consistently cleaned and reordered to enable fresh activity.

Order is also critical to my creative process. Because my visual-spatial mind races with a constant stream of thoughts, patterns, images and ideas, I need a strong sense of internal order. As a divergent thinker, I am constantly considering and reviewing numerous streams of information from a variety of sources for multiple possibilities. With this much mental activity going on, the ability to organize, sequence and structure is essential to my thought process. My mind would be an overwhelming jumble of chaotic information, without order, multi-step sequencing, and a disciplined thought process.

## Quiet

The ability to be silent is essential to my thought process. I understood that after my experience of learning to quiet myself and control my racing mind. I appreciated how Montessori was intentional in developing the ability to be silent and the pleasure of quiet in young children. As a child, art had allowed me endless hours spent in quiet, "lost in the moment" activity. Being thoroughly engaged in the task at hand, and one that brought me

quiet

such pleasure, helped me learn to tune out the "noise" in and around me. Quiet introspection and reflection enabled me to see and hear my thoughts.

Thinking and creating require a clear internal dialogue free from the distractions of the busyness surrounding us. One must be able to hear one's own inner thoughts in order to develop new lines of thinking. This kind of internal dialogue and inner connectedness is a critical component of creativity that spans all disciplines, and is a behavior that must be *intentionally* developed.

## Patterning & Differentiation

Differentiation skills, key to success in education, are about seeing patterns and noticing differences. Through consistent participation in activities designed to develop patterning and discrimination skills, children acquire key thinking and learning abilities. The materials and activities in the Montessori classroom were ripe with sequencing activities, based on the observation of patterns by size, gradients or repetitions. Reading, writing and math are all pattern-based, requiring children to see patterns and discern critical differences. As they gain patterning experience, they can begin to predict and anticipate next steps. Success in science, statistics, logic, engineering and computer programming require the ability to sequence, discern, anticipate, create, hypothesize and predict.

Patterning ability is critical to success in all core subjects, but its direct impact can be difficult to measure. Music is a pattern-based discipline, often credited with increasing math skills, hence the "Mozart Effect". Mathematical ability is more easily quantified, which may explain why the connection between music and math has been identified. Musical training is a multisensory experience that trains children to think, hear and move kinesthetically in sequences and patterns. When children learn to read music, they are reading visual patterns. With consistent instruction and exposure to music, their minds are trained to hear, think and see patterns. With this core competency in place, they apply these patterning abilities to other subjects.

Once I understood the impact of sequencing and patterning skills on the thinking process, I considered the ways my own mind processed patterns. As a visual person, I am constantly observing patterns. Being visual, seeing is my primary mode of thinking and processing. As I perceive the world around me, my mind categorizes shapes, sizes, colors, textures, values, relationships, proportions and scales. Being an art kid, I was even more attracted to patterns, observing them in objects, shapes, people and even the situations around me. The visual arts use visual elements — line, texture, color and shapes — to create patterns and themes that unify compositions. Music uses reoccurring tempos, rhythms and melodies to connect and unify a composition.

> " *All forms of the arts — visual art, music, dance and theater — provide opportunities to develop essential visual, spatial, sequencing, patterning and differentiation abilities...* "

Just as Montessori education engaged multisensory experiences to help young children develop and internalize skills critical to future learning and thinking, the arts offer this same opportunity. All forms of the arts — visual art, music, dance and theater — provide opportunities to develop essential visual, spatial, sequencing, patterning and differentiation abilities, which undergird crucial learning functions. It turns out that being visual and artistic had given me a distinct advantage. Along with strengthening my ability to learn, being able to see physical and visual patterns helped me sort, order, organize and create cohesiveness. Having strong pattern and differentiation skills enabled me to identify and connect divergent thoughts, come up with new ideas and be creative. But it was not just about the arts; I realized these abilities had helped me in other academic areas like reading, math and science.

## The Science of Building a Mind

Years after my time around Montessori education, I stumbled upon a field of research that confirmed what I had observed in the classroom. One evening at our son's school, I met Kenneth A. Wesson, an Education Consultant of Neuroscience, who opened my eyes to learning strategies based on the latest scientific research. Wesson lectures all over the globe, sharing the latest research with educators in an effort to help develop brain-friendly learning environments. I attended the lecture as a parent, but listened as an educator. After his lengthy and detailed presentation, I realized many of the research studies and recommended teaching strategies he shared were in alignment with Montessori education.

I waited to speak with Mr. Wesson, excited to ask questions and gain further clarity. First, I asked his opinion on Dr. Montessori's theories. He replied, "Brilliant. Everything she observed 100 years ago is now being proven scientifically." He then proceeded to share specific ways children's brains were affected while learning and affirmed the value of specific teaching techniques for pre-school and visual-spatial students.

In the days and weeks that followed, I began reading Wesson's materials, the works of researchers and other education and learning specialists. Montessori considered the first six years of life critical in a child's development, coining the phrase the "absorbent mind." Scientists agree and have documented that "neural networks by which all future complex learning will be based are forged during this critical early period and by a specific series of vitally important brain processes."[50] Children are born with millions, possibly billions, of neurons and connection opportunities in their brains. When these neurons are used they sprout connections, called dendrites. These dendrites are vitally important to the flow of information through the brain, whether it concerns the storage of a memory or a physical task, like walking or drawing.

Thick masses of dendrites create "dendrite forests" and young children are set with the task of developing these neural connections, as their minds are being sculpted into the brain it will become. The early years of a child's life are enormously significant developmentally, because the more the brain is stimulated, the more dendrites are developed and connected.[51] This creates the structure for all future learning.

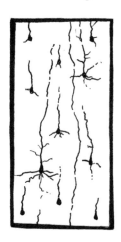 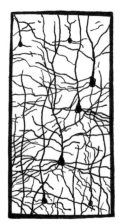

In the early stages of this development, a child's brain is typically working at 225%, the energy level of adults and is incredibly adept at gathering and understanding new information.[52] This coincides with Montessori's view of the child as a sponge, eagerly seeking out and absorbing information and experiences. It also reminds us of how ripe young children are for learning and the care we must take in providing them the appropriate stimulation and information.

Science has proven that the human brain is a very efficient machine, and if a child's brain is not adequately stimulated during this time, many healthy brain cells will disappear, callously trimmed away by the brain due to under use — the "use it or lose it" phenomenon. In a Harvard Eye Study (1963)[53], researchers used newborn kittens to demonstrate the effect of sensory deprivation. Kittens were unable to use one eye, because it was sewn closed at birth. After several weeks, the eye was reopened to find it had lost its ability to see. Brain cells won't survive the pruning process if they don't find a job to do during critical periods of development.

As the child's brain searches out experiences and information about the world around them, the brain deconstructs it, sending the information to different parts of the brain. When the child later needs to use the information, the brain recalls and reassembles it after comparing it to other stored data. As a pattern-seeking device, the brain is always on the lookout for patterns that help organize and make sense of the stored data. The more experiences a child has, the bigger the database the child's brain builds and, therefore, more information and patterns will be available for future use in learning and queries.

## Memory & Remembering

The actual structure of the brain is physically changed when new learning occurs. Neuroscience has demonstrated there's a distinctly different structure to the pre-reading brain when compared to the brain that can read. During the pre-reading phase, the brain is tasked with building dendrite connections through visual, tactile, auditory and kinesthetic experiences. The more extensive and comprehensive the child's experiences are, the more dendrite connections are formed. All children are building a database from multisensory experiences, but this is especially significant for our visual-spatials, who will largely rely on their visual database.

As visual, tactile and auditory information comes in, the brain deconstructs the data and analyzes each part of the experience independently. For example, when a child sees and touches a red ball, the brain takes note of the color red, the roundness of ball, its size, weight and texture, along with the any related sounds or language. Every element of that experience is filed in different parts of the brain.

The process of building the mental reference library through sensory experiences, and later accessing stored information, are two separate and distinct mental functions. Once a child learns to read, the brain function shifts. Instead of inputting as much data, it will retrieve data from the database of information previously developed. For example, when the child is reading and encounters the word "ball," the brain will pull the information it needs to understand "ball" from separate areas of the brain. It will remember the color, feel, sound, size and any other details of the experience. This process is repeated over and over as the child reads, and the depth of database that's been built will have a direct impact on reading success.

## Drawing from the Database

Once, when completing a writing and drawing assignment for second grade English class, our daughter Liz came asking for help. She had written a story and needed to draw a fire engine to illustrate it. First, we looked for a picture in a book, so she could see the fire engine's basic shapes. None were to be found, and it was pre-home computers. So without a visual reference to look at, we talked it out. Liz was an experienced artist who had seen real fire engines and pictures of fire engines.

I asked her, "What is the overall shape?"

She thought a moment and answered, "A long rectangle."

"Where is the line that divides the front cab section from the rear?"

"By the front," she said.

"How many wheels are on each side?"

"Two."

"Okay," I said. "Let's talk about the front cab section. What shape is the window?"

"Square."

"What shape is the door?" I asked.

"Rectangle."

"Who will you see up front?"

"The fireman driving," she replied.

"Now, let's talk about the back section," I continued. "What kinds of things are attached to the back?"

"Hoses, ladders, dials and knobs," Liz said.

"What shape is the ladder?"

"Two long skinny rectangles with lines across."

"How would you draw the hose?" I asked.

"A big circle with circle lines inside," Liz replied.

As she described the details her confidence grew, and with the fire engine clearly in her mind's eye, Liz went back to her desk to finish her work. Later, she reappeared beaming with pride. Her assignment was complete and included a perfect drawing of a very detailed fire engine, the firemen, the road and clouds on a bright, sunny day.

## Needing Sensory Input

Our visual-spatial children need visuals to learn, but it seems science, like Montessori 100 years ago, is telling us that all learning abilities are deeply affected by the style and quantity of visual, tactile and auditory experiences. From birth to six-years-old, children have been busy building a database, a reference library in their minds. But while the brain may shift functions to read stored data, it will always require visual, tactile and auditory data input. Receiving, analyzing, categorizing and storing information sensorially is a constant, natural, essential brain function. It's how our minds are wired. It's how we are in pre-school, how we'll be in formal education settings, and how we'll be the rest of our lives.

Researchers have described the three separate and distinct ways the mind receives, stores and shares information as: schematic, procedural and semantic. *Schematic processing* involves the use of visual images and pictures. *Procedural knowledge* refers to information gained through the use of movement and motor skills. *Semantic processing* refers to language, which includes auditory and verbal language skills.

As human beings, we are all innately visual, physical and auditory beings. Babies are born with the ability to see. It's instinctive. Their schematic, visual skills are their primary source of interacting with the world. They are also naturally attuned to sound, touch, temperature and texture. Gross motor skills keep us moving for a lifetime of activity that's an essential part of our being and the foundation of our procedural processing skills. Sound takes on new meaning as children begin to understand and communicate through spoken language, the foundation of semantic processing.

## Visual, Auditory & Kinesthetic Learning (VAK)

Along with auditory-sequential and visual-spatial learners, another model of learning styles reflects three modes of sensory processing: visual, auditory and kinesthetic learning (VAK).

> *Visual learning* corresponds to visual-spatial learning. It involves the use of things that are seen and, much like schematic processing, involves the use of visual images and pictures.
>
> *Auditory learning*, like auditory-sequential learning, involves the transfer of information through hearing sounds, words, and self-speech, including the tradition of oral language.
>
> *Kinesthetic learning* involves the physical body and includes touching, feeling and doing, much like procedural processing uses information gained through the use of movement and motor skills.

The philosophy of visual, auditory and kinesthetic learning styles aligns with researchers' findings on schematic, procedural and kinesthetic methods of processing information. It also speaks to the value early childhood educators, like Montessori, placed on multisensory learning experiences for young children and underscores what scientists have documented about the brain's method of assimilating and storing information in the developmental years. While individuals use a combination of these three learning modalities, they tend to favor one over the others, resulting in visual, auditory and kinesthetic learners.

## Kinesthetic Learners

Kinesthetic learners are also known as tactile learners. While there are great similarities, tactile learners do best when touching and doing, while kinesthetic learners enjoy the addition of physical activity. These hands-on learners can get restless in the classroom, and their need to move may lead some to think they are hyperactive. They work well with their hands, have strong hand-eye coordination and strong motor memory. When learning includes movement or use of their body, they remember by recalling what their body was doing.

Teaching that is heavily driven by lecture is difficult for the kinesthetic learner. Listening is not enough. These kids need ways to keep their bodies engaged. Kinesthetic learners do better when moving while listening, the use of manipulatives, doodling, taking notes, building dioramas, making models and participation in role-play. They prefer science labs to science class, play sports, do art, theater and pursue activities that involve the use of their body.

All of this doing also involves seeing. While it's impossible for classroom teachers to adapt every lesson for the three different types of learners, there are many similarities between visual and kinesthetic learning needs. Most importantly, the majority of our kids need to do more than listen. They need to see, touch and do

**4**

to learn. Teaching that includes mixed modality presentations — visual, auditory and kinesthetic techniques — will improve outcomes for all students.

## Deficiency & Potential

When children enter elementary school, they enter an education system centered on linguistic and logic skills. In kindergarten, young children are allowed to move and use some sensory tools to learn, but by first grade, they're told to sit still, face forward, listen, read and write. Traditional teaching styles are heavily language, logic and memory focused. IQ tests, standardized testing and classroom exams measure and evaluate these limited aspects of intelligence, overlooking the vastness of their individual abilities.

Over the years, the amount of valuable classroom instruction time devoted to testing has increased dramatically. Standardized testing is now used in such excess that it rules the education process. Test results drive funding and determine curriculum. With so much at stake for schools, teaching to tests has increased, lessening instruction in other "less relevant" subject areas. The subjects getting funded are the ones getting tested; they are linear, logical, linguistic subjects. It's a vicious cycle that isn't working for most children.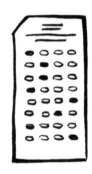

Sadly, this has had a profound effect on our children and education as a whole. We're in an education gridlock. Teachers know it. Parents know it. Kids know it. Testing increasingly drives what's happening in our classrooms, yet our test scores are not getting any better. There's an enormous disservice being done to our students whose true capabilities are going unnoticed and undeveloped. Teachers are frustrated. Parents are baffled. Kids are bored. Classrooms grow duller while ADD and ADHD are on the rise.

Our kids don't get to move around enough anymore. They don't get to use their bodies, touch what they are learning, build, make, see or do. They sit in chairs focused on reading, writing and math because they're being tested on reading, writing and math. The more our schools focus on this restricted skill set, the less room there is for alternate teaching methods and a broader range of subject matter.

When budget cuts force school districts to cut programs, opportunities get scarcer. And yet the programs that are being cut are the very ones that allow children to fully engage in the learning process. Subjects such as art, music, band and gym engage children visually, tactilely and kinesthetically. These subjects represent the intelligences that have been left behind, neglected and unnoticed. These subjects also carry with them the potential for children to perform better in reading, writing and math. These are the subjects that engage children in ways that develop those "learning to learn" skills, critical to all thinking and learning processes.

## Many Kinds of Smart

Once our kids were in elementary school, I wondered about the disconnect between the structured sensory learning that had been so successful and the shift to sitting in chairs, learning from lecture, books and worksheets. Once in school, their ability to learn became about grades. They were measured by grades on class assignments, tests and homework. Evaluating their intelligence through testing began and life became A, B, C or "none of the above". While all our children did well in school, I wondered how report cards, IQ, SAT and ACT scores could possibly reflect all they were capable of. Measurement is useful, but as sensory beings, how was school accounting for the broader spectrum of their skill and ability?

When looking for answers, I came upon the work of Howard Gardner. In 1983, Gardner, a professor at Harvard University, proposed the theory of multiple intelligences. He felt the way IQ tests measured intelligence did not accurately

or sufficiently reflect the wide variety of cognitive abilities people possess. Gardner challenged the idea of intelligence as a single entity and believed people were a unique blend of intelligences, with dominance in one or two areas. These intelligences are used simultaneously, but each has its own unique strength and limitation. He noted that people operate every day with a multitude of abilities, which correlate to their distinctive blend of intelligences.

Gardner identified eight basic types of intelligence: spatial, linguistic, logical-mathematical, kinesthetic, musical, interpersonal, intrapersonal and naturalist.[54]

*Intrapersonal* intelligence signals keen self-reflective and introspective capabilities. Individuals with high intrapersonal intelligence have strong intuitive skills and a deep understanding of self.

*Spatial* learners are visual. They learn best with pictures, have strong spatial awareness along with the ability to recognize and use patterns.

*Interpersonal* intelligence reflects the ability to interact with others, an understanding of intentions and motivation, resulting in strong social and relationship skills.

*Linguistic* learners have strong language skills. They use both written and spoken words to express themselves and remember information. Most teachers have high linguistic intelligence.

*Logical-mathematical* thinkers detect patterns, reason deductively and think logically. They learn well though numbers and reasoning.

*Kinesthetic* students learn best through movement. They handle objects well, including their own physical bodies.

*Musical* intelligence is closely related to logical-mathematical thinking. These thinkers have strong auditory skills and are sensitive to sound, rhythms, music and musical patterns.

*The Naturalist* is very aware of nature. They learn best when relating information to their surroundings.

## It's All Connected

I was excited to see the connection among sensory learning, left and right-brain thinking and the abilities represented in the intelligences Gardner described. Gardner's work also confirmed the connection between spatial intelligence and visual skills. Both musical and linguistic intelligence have auditory strengths, and kinesthetic intelligence is related to physical movement and the use of one's body in space, like sports and dance. I also noticed how these intelligences acknowledged specific skills Montessori educated children develop — patterning, sequencing, logical thought, even the ability to be quiet and hear one's own thoughts.

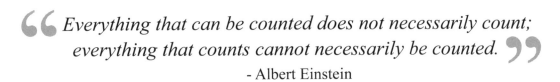

*Everything that can be counted does not necessarily count; everything that counts cannot necessarily be counted.*
- Albert Einstein

Understanding Gardner's theories gave me a broader, more encompassing view of my children and myself. I felt a sense of enhanced value. These abilities and areas of strength mattered. Schools couldn't measure them and weren't always using them to teach and engage, but that didn't mean they weren't there or weren't valuable. Albert Einstein said, "Everything that can be counted does not necessarily count; everything that counts cannot necessarily be counted." I thought about how much we could empower our young learners by providing a more holistic view of their intelligence and giving them back confidence lost by low test scores.

Gardner's theory of multiple intelligences has been well-accepted by some educators, giving rise to differentiated teaching strategies designed to acknowledge differences and adapt teaching methods. We need to break the reliance on standardized testing, teaching to tests and thinking tests are the measure of successful teaching and knowledge acquisition. There is enormous potential for teaching methods, curriculum and tools that move beyond the logical, linguistic tests, textbooks and worksheets currently being used and for re-engaging the senses. A multisensory approach to learning brings with it the opportunity to re-engage our weary learners, as we create ways to meet our students in their areas of strength and innate ability.

## Sit Still & Read!

Our son's high school English teacher had advanced degrees and a love of literature. Yet, it was virtually impossible for even the best students to do well in his class. This frustrated most of the parents and made for repeated attempts to change his teaching methods, which was usually met with a suggestion that students be more focused and try harder.

When it was time for our first parent-teacher conferences, it became apparent that the teacher, while an expert in literature, did not understand learning styles. In our case, along with being a visual learner, our son is very much a kinesthetic learner. Like many  boys, as a young child, he was always in motion and loved almost any type of physical play. He loved using his hands and moving his body. He started playing sports at age five, and played on a variety of athletic teams all throughout school.

When we met to talk about English class and Matt's performance, his teacher suggested Matt end his participation in after school sports. He thought the sooner he got home to study, the more time he could spend reading and writing papers.

Knowing how much Matt needed physical activity, we explained that even without sports, he would never be the kid that hurried home to read or write papers. After a long day of sitting in classrooms, he looked forward to afternoon sport practices and the opportunity to be physical. After time spent being active and the release of built up energy, he could sit again and focus on homework. Unfortunately, the class and this teacher's methods never changed, but I hoped our conversation brought some helpful insight.

# Everybody Can

It was fall, the time for kids to be back to school and after-school programs to begin again. I was working in the Young Rembrandts offices, helping get the school year off to a successful start. We had recently hired a new group of instructors and, having been an instructor myself, I had the pleasure of helping new teachers start their first classes. I had been a long-time Young Rembrandts student as a child and now was the one helping the kids see shapes and apply color. All throughout class, I enjoyed their smiles and steady concentration, but the best part of class on this Thursday afternoon was a boy named Frank.

Frank was a child with high-functioning autism. His mother had enrolled him in the class with some concern about his ability to participate. When class first started, Frank was a little rambunctious, waving his hands and bouncing in his chair. He had some difficulty focusing and seemed a bit uncomfortable with the other children. As we got further into the lesson, he calmed down. His focus wandered a bit between steps but, for the most part, Frank was as engaged, calm and collected as the rest of the children. He did really well and seemed to enjoy his time drawing and coloring.

Later, while helping a child to the washroom, I came across a mom in the hallway, quietly watching our class. The tears in her eyes were enough to tell me she was Frank's mom. A flood of questions and instructions came pouring out of her. "How is he doing? Is he behaving? Just say 'quiet hands' if he gets to be too much…" I assured her everything was fine, he was well-behaved and doing very well in class. A sense of peace come over her as she realized that her Frank, even with his learning challenges, was able to focus, be part of a group and be an artist just like the rest of the children.

- Liz Fetter
*Director of Marketing, Young Rembrandts*

# 5

# Special Opportunities

5

55

66 She is different, not less. 99
- Eustacia Cutler[55]

I**N THE PROCESS OF UNDERSTANDING** visual-spatial learning needs and teaching my own structured art classes, I have become aware of ways visual teaching strategies work well with other groups of individuals. Children with autism, Asperger's and special needs benefit from instruction that is highly visual, hands-on and less language-focused. They also benefit from a structured, predictable learning process that includes carefully segmented and ordered steps.

We also used visual teaching strategies, specifically Young Rembrandts drawing classes, to teach seniors recovering from strokes, seniors with early stage dementia and seniors in the early stages of Alzheimer's. In each circumstance, several key elements of our visual teaching method were effective in meeting these individuals in their unique place of need. While we have no definitive scientific studies to explain exactly why it all worked, I would like to share their stories.

## Children with Autism

Autism is a spectrum disorder. There are some consistencies of needs and ways to process stimuli, but there are also vast variations of ways autism presents, hence, the term "spectrum". Children with autism tend to have stronger visual-spatial

> ❝ *"One of the most profound mysteries of autism has been the remarkable ability of most autistic people to excel at visual spatial skills while performing so poorly at verbal skills."* ❞

skills and weaker verbal abilities. In her book, *Thinking in Pictures, My Life with Autism*, Temple Grandin, a successful high-functioning adult with autism, shares, "One of the most profound mysteries of autism has been the remarkable ability of most autistic people to excel at visual spatial skills while performing so poorly at verbal skills." Temple goes on to outline three categories of autistic thinkers:

"1. *Visual thinkers*, like me, think in photographically specific images. There are degrees of specificity in visual thinking. I can test run a machine in my head with full motion. Interviews with non-autistic, visual thinkers indicated that they can only visualize still images.

2. *Music and Math thinkers* think in patterns. These people excel in math, chess and computer programming. Some of these individuals explained to me that they see patterns and relationships between patterns and numbers instead of photographic images. Written language is not required for pattern thinking.

3. *Verbal logic thinkers* think in word details. They often love history, foreign languages, weather statistics, and stock market reports. They are not visual thinkers and are often poor at drawing. Children with speech delays are more likely to become visual or music math thinkers."[56]

The descriptions Grandin provides are very similar to descriptions of visual-spatial and auditory-sequential thinkers, along with the math distinction provided by multiple intelligences. As a group, students with autism are much more focused on detail. Temple is clearly a visual thinker, but instead of the usual conceptual strength of the traditional visual-spatial thinker, she is very detail-oriented. Researcher Nancy Minshew, at Carnegie Mellon University in Pittsburg, has found that "normal brains tend to ignore details while people on the autism spectrum tend to focus on details instead of larger concepts." In her study, Minshew found autistic brains focused on individual words, normal brains analyzed whole sentences, and the Asperger brain was active in both areas.[57] Students with autism can also have a variety of sensory processing difficulties, with extreme oversensitivity in some sensory areas.

Paula Kluth, Ph.D., is an educator and advocate working with students with autistic and special needs. In her book, *The Autism Checklist, A Practical Reference for Parents and Teachers*, Kluth gives advice on home and school support for children with autism and Asperger's syndrome. She suggests instructions need to include show-and-tell examples, step-by-step directions and the use of icons or pictures to enhance understanding. She also talks about the need to avoid overloading

> 66 *... 'normal brains tend to ignore details while people on the autism spectrum tend to focus on details instead of larger concepts.'* 99

students with verbal language and their need for predictable routines. "Structure (learning) units as predictably as you can... Create daily and weekly rituals that all students can look forward to... break assignments into meaningful chunks."[58]

## More than Expected

Recently, we received a call from a parent whose child was taking Young Rembrandts classes. This mom, Michelle, who calls herself an "autism advocate," called to say how much the classes were benefiting her son. Seven-years-old now, her son was diagnosed with autism at 18 months and was told he would always be low functioning. But after many years of education and special therapies, he is now classified with high functioning autism.

When Michelle first saw the Young Rembrandts enrollment flyer, she dismissed it, calling herself an "art snob." As a child, she was not allowed to trace, use coloring books, color in the lines or anything that might stifle her creativity, so the thought of enrolling her son in a structured art class didn't appeal to her. Eventually, she reconsidered her decision and thought the class could be a good experience for him, not for the art, but for the social interaction. She readily said, "I didn't expect good instruction and didn't care." She wanted the social interaction and the ability to assess him in an after school environment.

Michelle enrolled her son in a session of eight classes and attended the first class to observe him in the group setting. She wanted to be sure he was comfortable and doing well. What she experienced was not what she anticipated. Much to her own surprise, she enjoyed the instruction the teacher was sharing with the young students and felt she was learning along with them. She noticed her son modeling positive peer behavior; he seemed to feel good about the class overall, and she was "floored" by his level of participation and engagement in the learning process. He completed the drawing and coloring was very pleased and ready to return the following week.

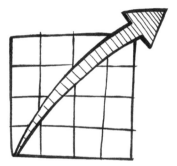

Michelle's own beliefs about the way to teach art were powerfully affected by her observations. She enrolled her son in our program, not expecting anything from the education, but was most impressed by the educational process. She reconsidered the notion that giving information and using tools to learn art would stifle creativity. Involvement in her son's education had made her keenly aware of his need to learn in an orderly, sequential, visual, step-by-step progression, and she saw how the class provided this structure for him.

## Why It Worked

Many of the teaching adaptations that are effective for visual learners are also effective with autistic learners. Children with

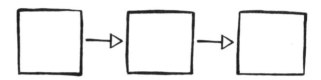

autism are prompt, dependent and function better in structured situations that incorporate visual and tactile opportunities. They need visual cues, need to be told what to do (instead of what not to do), be provided examples and models, and have the pace of the class meet their level of process and understanding. The instructor's language needs to be brief, directive and literal.

Children with autism can also be challenged by social interaction. They are highly sensitive to sensory stimuli, and social settings can be overwhelming. These students often interact and connect differently and need collaborative activities that allow them to be with others in a social setting, but require less face-to-face time or direct interaction with peers. The structured Young Rembrandts art classroom allowed them to work side-by-side, in a regulated setting, with less direct peer interaction.

The quiet and absence of extraneous dialogue in our classrooms was also helpful for students with autism who struggle with sensory overload. An art class with visual clues and organized step-by-step instruction allowed children to control their listening mode. Having visuals full of direction and information allowed them to look at the static images, rather than an instructor's face or other distracting stimuli. Since the majority of our instruction was visual and less language-dependent, students were less distracted overall, able to focus on the task at hand.

Art, specifically drawing, is a form of controlled communication. If a child with autism has difficulty with receptive language or sharing himself or herself verbally, drawing provides them a unique outlet. When children draw they can tell their story, communicating thoughts and moods without language. They may also find comfort in the ability to control the pace and structure of communication, especially if they feel they have less control in other areas. Sharing through drawing has value in and of itself, but it's also preparation for communicating thoughts through language. This is true of all learners who are developing their communication and language capabilities.

> " *Art, specifically drawing, is a form of controlled communication.* "

Our instructors have many success stories to share, and we're excited to find more and more children with autism participating in our weekly classes. We look forward to expanding our reach and furthering our own understanding of this talented, special group of students.

## Special Needs

It's estimated that over 6 million children in the United States (roughly 10% of school-aged children) receive some form of special education services. Special education serves children with behavioral and learning challenges, and emotional, physical and developmental disorders. Special needs teachers are trained to assess student-learning needs and adapt teaching methods for their students. Instructional strategies include adaptations to the way material is presented, along with ways for children to learn self-management techniques and impulse control. Students also experience a level of safety and comfort when they know what to expect next. They need structure, routine and predictability in their activities, and perform better in situations that provide a logical progression of activity, along with predictability of next steps.

## Drawing with Special Teens

One summer, a friend of mine contacted us about teaching a four-week program for her special needs students. Barb and I were friends through church, and when she heard that our teaching method relied heavily on the use of a visual, step-by-step process, she felt it would be appropriate for her special students. Art classes were held at this particular high school, but students of special education weren't able to participate. Barb, the lead teacher, didn't have any expectations of great art being done, but wanted to incorporate some new activities in her summer school program. This group of students ranged from 14 to 18 years of age and had a variety of cognitive delays, including some teens with autism. They had second and third grade reading levels, IQ's in the 50 to 70 range and some had significant physical handicaps.

Our instructor, Molly, who is also a trained special education teacher, was not sure what to expect when she arrived at the first class. But her background and previous training led her to prepare for class by scaling the lesson to match their anticipated attention span and understanding level. As the instructor entered class, she met Barb and several of her classroom aides. Molly began class as she usually does and proceeded to introduce the lesson to the students. When the classroom aides and teacher saw what the students were going to draw, there was some concern they were headed for failure that would lead to emotional upset, rather than the positive experience they hoped for. But they decided to trust the instructor, watched patiently and helped as the class and activity evolved.

Molly introduced the lesson, talking about the animal they were going to draw, giving background information and showing pictures of where it lived. The first lesson was a sea turtle, and the students seemed interested and were responding well. She asked simple questions to engage them, keeping her language simple, clear and straightforward, rephrasing words or concepts when needed. With paper and pencils distributed, and aides helping children position the paper appropriately, the drawing portion of class began. The instructor used the same visual, step-by-step process of instruction that she used in Young Rembrandts pre-school classes.

 She drew and explained each part of the sea turtle as they proceeded to draw it. They used their hands to measure and gauge size, and their fingers to help with placement on the page. Aides helped students make shapes or directed them back to task when needed. They responded well and seemed to appreciate the structure and ability to anticipate the next steps. As the drawing portion of class was complete, each child paused to look at the drawing on their page. Their images were large, complete and filled the entire page, with some added scene details.

When it was time to color, Molly used simple language to explain the coloring process while visually demonstrating basic coloring techniques. Again, the students responded well to the structure and explanation of the process. They liked the order, the steps and the information on how to do the coloring. The amount of care and skill used in coloring was remarkable. Students without strong fine motor skills applied color more lightly than other students, but did complete their entire piece. Even the students with physical handicaps completed their entire drawing, proud to have been in art class.

After the forty-five minute class, students were ready to move to their next classroom activity, anxious to stay in their daily routine. Every student completed the entire lesson, all the drawing and all the coloring steps. They were quite pleased with themselves, able to identify and name the shapes used to draw their sea turtle and happy to show off their masterpieces. A couple of students asked when they would do more art. Barb and her assistants were delighted by the work their students did and the level they were able to achieve. Students with a wide range of special needs were 100% engaged throughout the class with no outbursts, no distractions and no discipline issues. The series of classes continued on for three more weeks, for a total of four lessons. Students participated in art lessons that met them at their unique level of physical and cognitive ability, and each week, the same level of success happened in the classroom.

## Why It Worked

When I asked Barb why she thought our teaching method was so successful with her students, she compared it to other special needs teaching strategies. The class used plenty of visuals, minimal language and sequential and predictable tasks. The order and structure of our drawing process, along with visual presentation of material and step-by-step process, made it something they could relate to and understand. Barb thought our lessons were "chunked" well, referring to the lesson introduction, learning to see the shapes, and then the drawing and coloring. Chunking, the process of delivering information in smaller bite size pieces, reduces the cognitive load, and allows better understanding and absorption of material. In actuality, all students perform better when information is chunked, because the brain can only hold a limited amount of information at a given time.

After the classroom success, Barb and her aides were very interested in their students continuing to participate in these types of classes. But school budgets were tight, and the funding was not available for ongoing programs. Our hope is to find ways to incorporate this teaching method in special education classrooms and provide ways for these children to learn visually, develop fine motor and key learning skills, as well as the pleasure of participating in the arts.

## Drawing with Special Young Ones

There's an elementary school with an on site pre-school, located near our corporate offices. The program serves at-risk pre-school children with severe emotional issues, developmental delays and Down syndrome. We conducted some test classes at the school and by making slight adjustments to our delivery methods, found them able to participate like other groups of "normal" pre-school students. To thank the school for allowing us to work with their young students, we offered them one year of complementary, weekly Young Rembrandts classes. This allowed us to further test our assumption that our teaching methodology would work effectively with all children.

Each of the weekly classes included fifteen students, ranging from 3-1/2 to 5-1/2 year olds, one trained Young Rembrandts instructor and classroom aides helping where needed. Each week our instructor, an experienced special education teacher, brought in a Young Rembrandts pre-school lesson and taught it to the class. As a strong instructor, the teacher was playful and engaging as she presented the lesson material and worked through the week's lesson. She made slight adjustments to curriculum and materials, knowing there were some developmental and emotional challenges. Thicker pencils were used to draw and crayons were used to color.

Even though the lessons were simplified, there were still some students able to complete more advanced level work. The children responded well to the Young Rembrandts classroom techniques, and everyone participated fully in class. Students with Down syndrome were able to participate with the help of their aides. From time to time, one or two children had a brief emotional struggle, and the classroom aide stepped in to help them through it. But these times were rare. Overall, the weekly class progressed like every other Young Rembrandts pre-school class with each student making strides relative to their innate level of ability.

After some initial concern about the students' ability to be attentive and stay on task in this type of setting, the school staff enjoyed watching their students participate in the weekly classes. They were consistently amazed to see all fifteen kids gathered around the classroom tables ready, focused and excited to participate. Teachers and aides would sometimes watch the class to observe the classroom techniques the Young Rembrandts instructor was using, delighted to see the students follow directions, put pencils down when asked, write their names and ask for help when needed. Drawing and coloring skills increased over time, and language skills seemed to increase as well.

After the series of classes was complete, our instructor evaluated the effectiveness of the program in this setting. She shared, "We truly measured our success with their ability to follow all directions, get the initial shape down and recognize that our picture was made up of basic shapes. The real successes of this program were that it was held during school hours, all children came ready to learn and they all demonstrated increased abilities."

## Children in Crisis

On several occasions, we have been asked to teach at facilities that serve hard-to-place kids from families in crisis. At one of these schools, we've been teaching a program for children six to fourteen-year-olds with mild to moderate emotional or behavioral challenges. The school had a very limited budget, so to provide classes for their students, they found a business partner to help with funding. Once that round of funding expired, they wanted to continue the program and were fortunate to be sponsored by their community art club.

Young Rembrandts classes at this facility have been following the curriculum and teaching methods used in all other classrooms. The children have been participating fully, and a special bulletin board proudly displays their art work. After a series of classes, the staff reported a notable improvement in the individual student's attention span and time on task. Staff members have also commented on the students' increased fine motor control and ability to focus. Their listening skills and willingness to follow directions have affected other areas of learning. As one staff member said, "These students are used to having no expectations. But they're going from 'I can't to I can,' and they're thinking better about themselves."

When one young student was asked for permission to use his drawing in a local display, he was pleased his work had been chosen. With generosity of spirit, he gave permission to take his talent and fame to the next level when he shared, "If you can sell it, feel free!"

## Seniors with Alzheimer's

Alzheimer's is a heartbreaking disease that affects over 26 million seniors worldwide. Alzheimer's, the most common form of dementia, causes nerves in the brain to die, leading to tissue loss throughout the brain. This disrupts communication between the brain cells, affecting memory, speech and comprehension abilities. Early stage patients with Alzheimer's can have problems with short-term memory, organizing thoughts and expressing themselves. Later stages of Alzheimer's include problems with abstract thinking and other intellectual and memory functions.

Young Rembrandts was contacted by a facility in Florida that provides independent, medical and assisted living care for seniors. They had several seniors who needed more care after moving from assisted living into the medical unit. Many of these seniors had early Alzheimer's and the director wanted an activity that might help them maintain memory and mental function.

## Drawing with the Ladies

Six to eight ladies gathered each week for class. These adult students looked forward to activities and were delighted to attend. When class began and the subject matter was introduced, there was lively conversation, memories stirred and thoughts shared about that particular subject. Whether it was a basket of apples, a bird feeder or a pot of flowers, the opportunity for seeing, discussing and drawing seemed to help their memory, language and vocabulary skills.

The activity of drawing engaged the seniors, and the step-by-step drawing process was successful in leading them to completion each week. Perhaps as a response to their loss in memory and predictability, these seniors seemed to thrive on structure, guidance, and the step-by-step process. The opportunity for choice was welcome, the limited range comforting but not overwhelming. And while there was some confusion with paper orientation each week, following the instructor's directions proved to be a positive and calming experience.

The facility has been pleased with the program and has provided classes for several years now. Many seniors have participated, and while we have no clinical evidence to prove any change in mental function, they are reported to have enjoyed the conversation, the memories and the opportunity to make decisions about each new drawing.

## Senior Stroke Patients

Strokes affect the body and mind, and victims can suffer from impaired language skills, the inability to comprehend and use words, and have difficulty speaking and understanding others. A stroke occurs when the brain's blood supply is blocked, resulting in damage to parts of the brain. The effect of the stroke varies, depending on which area of the brain was damaged. It can cause impaired motor skills or a loss of cognitive function or intellectual abilities and difficulty paying attention, organizing tasks and trouble with visual orientation. Stroke rehabilitation efforts focus on regaining basic skills, which can vary depending on the severity of the stroke.

Recently, the mother of one of our long time Young Rembrandts instructors was moved to a nursing home to help her recover from a stroke. This instructor, Laurie, visited often and noticed her mother and patients with similar conditions needed help rebuilding their language skills. She requested permission to teach Young Rembrandts classes at the nursing home, thinking they could be helpful in the same ways drawing classes helped build vocabulary skills in young children. The classes would also provide some much needed activity. The classes had more impact than expected.

## Stirring Up Memories

Laurie, the instructor, approached this group of seniors with the expectation of helping them regain some of their fine motor abilities, language skills and memory function. For her first class, Laurie taught our fan lesson. She brought a hand held fan to class to give meaning to the visual concept, as she would in a class with young children. While introducing the lesson, she talked about the fan and asked questions to stimulate conversation. This was an opportunity to revive vocabulary and language skills while analyzing different parts of the drawing. Amid conversation on the shapes, sizes and patterns they observed, the seniors talked about their own experiences with fans. Old memories were triggered, as they shared stories and talked about using fans to cool themselves, as well as ways to signal their interest in certain gentlemen.

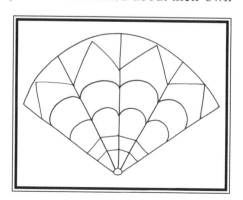

As Laurie taught the drawing class, she followed our usual step-by-step drawing method, and the seniors were happy to follow along, completing each step as she instructed. Once the basic fan shapes were in place, Laurie demonstrated line and pattern choices, and the seniors decorated their fans with the ideas that appealed to them. Throughout the class, the organization of tasks and orderly progression of steps seemed to have a calming effect on the group.

With drawings complete, Laurie explained and demonstrated the coloring process. When it was their turn to color, many of the seniors had difficulties with physical and fine motor skills, but they pressed on. Some were challenged to see the individual shapes in their drawings, much like our pre-school students had. The instructor used a typical Young Rembrandts technique, outlining the shape that needed to be colored in, then giving them back the marker so they could complete the coloring process independently. This process defined the space visually, allowing them the freedom and dignity of coloring in the space without further assistance. Each senior continued to color independently or with whatever level of assistance they required and completed the project, pleased with the activity and their finished drawings. This sequenced activity, designed to help rebuild language, visual and fine motor skills, had been a positive and much needed social experience.

> " *Drawing class was seen as an activity that gave back some of the dignity lost by circumstance.* "

While we have not conducted research to prove the results of our classes, we do have some simple observations. These seniors — bright, capable adults with vast life experiences, careers and families — have been humbled by stroke or disease. Seniors, especially under medical care and experiencing illness, live in situations very different than their previous lives. Many of their own personal choices have been removed: foods, daily schedules, medicine and recreation. Drawing class was seen as an activity that gave back some of the dignity lost by circumstance. It provided the opportunity to make independent choices, while including ways to regain understanding of the subject matter and to reconnect with past experiences. The activity of seeing, naming, drawing and coloring can help rebuild the mental database they established in their early years, the database that may have lost function and memory as a result of their illness. Overall, there was a level of participation, language and recall of past experience that gave great pleasure to the group.

## What's Next

Overall, Young Rembrandts remains focused on our work with pre-school and elementary students. We look forward to opportunities to further understand the impact and implications of our specialized drawing method and the value of visual-spatial teaching techniques for this special group of adults. We hope in the near future to participate in clinical research in order to clearly define the relationship between these unique learning needs and our methodology. In the meantime, children with ADD, ADHD, Asperger's and autism are able to participate successfully in our current class offerings.

# Before & After Young Rembrandts

Being an artist myself and armed with an art education degree, I began teaching art to elementary students right after graduating college. I carefully prepared my lesson plans and project samples, showed them to my students, demonstrated the process and then set them to work. I taught art the way I was trained to teach art, yet grew dissatisfied, feeling ill-prepared and not equipped to teach the skills I felt students needed to learn. I left the education community and used my own art skills to pursue a career in graphic design.

After many years as a successful graphic designer in corporate America, I longed to teach children again. I came across Young Rembrandts, a company that taught drawing classes after school, and became a part-time instructor while doing freelance design work. Young Rembrandts had a specific teaching method, focused on "how to draw" and seemed to address what I felt was missing in my early teaching career. After several years teaching children to draw with Young Rembrandts, I found myself ready for another career shift and decided to head back to the elementary school art classroom.

My experience with Young Rembrandts caused me to approach the elementary art classroom a bit differently. As before, I review the list of required artists, cultures and media for my grade levels. I decide what art concepts, techniques or processes I will cover throughout the year. But when I prepare my actual lessons, the time spent with Young Rembrandts becomes apparent. Now I include several additional steps in the preparation and teaching process, and am careful to include a series of visuals so students see the progression of steps we will be going through to complete the project. As I introduce each lesson, we spend time talking and relating the project to other art subjects, artists and cultures. And I break my classroom instruction into several smaller "chunks", being sure to give detailed, specific demonstration and step-by-step instructions so everyone can participate successfully.

Young Rembrandts has liberated me from the idea that "giving information" to students will stifle their creativity, so now I give plenty of instruction on drawing and media use. If a student draws the initial shapes too small on the page, they are redirected until they get the size and placement on the page correct, ensuring their success as the lesson progresses.

At this stage in my teaching career, I am no longer a "craft art teacher," but am a teacher focused on fine art and the development of foundational skills that include learning how to see and draw. I have also become increasingly aware of the impact my art classes have on my students' abilities in other subject areas.

- Carol Frueh
*Certified Elementary Art Teacher*
*& Young Rembrandts Instructor of 18 years*

# 6

**Teaching "How To"**

**6**

> " Drawing is really not very difficult. Seeing is the problem, or, to be more specific, shifting to a particular way of seeing. "
>
> - Betty Edwards[59]

Art has been and will always be essential to the human experience, yet it need not be limited to the small portion of the population that consider themselves artistic. The mind and skills that go into making art — seeing, doing, creating and considering multiple viewpoints — are the very skills used to create rich, full, satisfying lives. The world has become increasingly visual. Art, in all its forms, is a critical component of our future and it's essential that we understand its impact. We must teach art in ways that empower and create ways for art to infiltrate every aspect of our being.

The ability to see, draw and make visual symbols are key components of the visual literacy skills this generation needs. I was an art kid and a visual-spatial student, long before I knew there was a visual-spatial anything. Then an art student and artist. As a mother, I found Montessori education, or shall I say, it found me, igniting a life-long passion and interest in education. Eventually, this led me to teach art, a bit begrudgingly. This happened before I realized my life path had a purpose beyond myself. I thought teaching children how to draw was a temporary gig and just about art. Over the years I have come to see that while it is about art, it's also about using art to empower and equip our children for the future.

I started my teaching adventure with several young elementary students gathered around my kitchen table. Along the way I got to know what students could and could not do, and more importantly, *what they wanted to know* how to do. After some experience with elementary students, I taught classes at preschools, where I expanded my understanding of the needs of young students. Eventually "Bette's Art Classes" became Young Rembrandts. Using a carefully developed curriculum and a philosophy of best education practices to teach art, and more specifically, drawing, we now reach across the United States, Canada and the world. The Young Rembrandts teaching method combines the best of making art, with an informational, step-by-step, everyone-can-do-it approach. This journey to make a shift in the way we teach art has met with resistance from some parts of the education community, but its been minor compared to the welcome and success we have had along the way.

## Bette's Art Classes

After years spent working in the Montessori environment, a friend came to me with a request that set my life on another new course. It was 1988 and my friend, Christine, had been looking for art classes for her three elementary-aged children. They had their choice of music lessons, dance, gymnastics and sports of every flavor, but her kids wanted to learn how to draw. They had looked everywhere, but there were no art or drawing classes available in our area. When she first asked me to teach, I declined the invitation. I had absolutely no interest in teaching anyone how to draw.

My friend was very persistent, and as she continued to pursue the subject with me, I wondered why I was so hesitant. With a degree in art, professional graphic experience, my own time spent drawing, painting watercolors, and a passion for working with young children, it seemed I was the perfect candidate. But I didn't think I had anything to teach. I was never taught how to draw, and if it could be taught, then surely I would have gotten that kind of instruction. Maybe we aren't supposed to teach people how to draw. That had certainly been my experience. The more I thought about it, the more I remembered the consistent frustration and self-doubt that accompanied my lack of "how to" instruction, and I thought, perhaps there was a way.

Those unwavering memories and my friend's unrelenting encouragement finally wore me down. As a birthday gift to her, I agreed to teach drawing classes. Filled with lingering uncertainty, I gathered her children, a few more from the neighborhood including my older daughter, Laurie, and held my first class of eight students. Facing this small group sitting at my kitchen table, I wondered what I could teach them. I still wasn't sure how to teach drawing or if it was even the right thing to do, so I asked the kids what they wanted to know. It turned out they wanted to know the same things I wanted to know at their age. So I showed them.

Every week we met for art class, and every week, I showed them how to draw something. We drew people, faces, cars, animals — anything and everything. They named the subject matter or techniques they were interested in, and I gave them very specific "how to" instruction and demonstration. Week after week, we drew, their confidence and abilities steadily increasing, my understanding of their needs and interests growing. We had a lovely time together, all thriving on this exchange of information. Both students and parents were pleased and reported increased time spent drawing and coloring at home. Word about our classes got out, and more children joined us.

## Pre-School Drawing

Eventually, another friend, Jeanine, saw the drawings my students were doing. She thought the kids were drawing well beyond their years and asked about my classes.

She was a Montessori directress, and we had worked at the same Montessori school years before. Pleased with the explanation of what I was teaching my young elementary students, I was invited to offer my classes at the Montessori school that served three to five-year-olds in pre-school and day care programs. The school wanted to offer families additional educational opportunities aligned with their teaching philosophy. I was doubtful anyone would sign up for pre-school drawing classes, so with some hesitancy, I distributed enrollment flyers to their students. To my surprise I soon had a group of fourteen sweet little faces eager to learn.

Armed with an understanding of the Montessori teaching method, experience teaching elementary age students, and having studied various learning strategies, I faced my first class of pre-school students. I was intimidated — not by the young students — but by the task at hand. It was obvious that the way I was teaching elementary students how to draw would have to be adjusted to match the needs and abilities of these three, four and five-year-olds. Remembering how Montessori education used sandpaper letters to begin the learning to read process, and the bead and symbol work in math, I contemplated the beginning steps of learning to draw. After much thought, I carefully planned some lessons and headed into my first pre-school classes. Week after week, we drew and learned. In time, classroom experience helped shape theory into very successful applications.

## Learning to "See"

Each week, I arrived at the school, armed with a new lesson. Each week, my little ones gathered around the large table, anxious to learn. Once we were settled and focused on the task at hand, I brought out the object we were going to draw. I was careful to choose things that were in their realm of experience and things they might read about, like a teddy bear, bird's nest or butterfly. I showed it to the students, intentionally arousing their interest and curiosity. We would have a lovely chat about it, who used it and where it was to be found. Frontloading the lesson gave students the opportunity to place the object in context, further their own understanding of it, and develop vocabulary and language skills. Once we finished talking about our subject, we looked it over very thoroughly and identified key features, basic shapes, colors and patterns. This exercise was designed to heighten their observation and visual skills, and a way to be intentional about developing their pre-reading database and visual vocabulary.

> 66 *Doing this repeatedly helped children learn to see the basic shapes within complex objects, notice details, patterns and develop their visual acuity.* 99

Next, I showed the students a drawing of the same object. Again, we talked about it, carefully analyzing key shapes, features and its position on the page. This was wonderful time spent seeing — *really seeing*. Doing this repeatedly helped children learn to see the basic shapes within complex objects, notice details, patterns and develop their visual acuity. After time spent seeing, we looked at the same

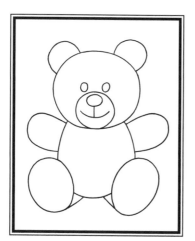

drawing, but this time it was filled with color. We went through the same process of really seeing the colors and how they affected the drawing. All of this observation and discussion happened before anyone ever touched paper or pencil. It provided them time to *see and think* about what they were going to draw *before they started*. Along with building their visual vocabularies, it allowed them to see the three-dimensional object before it became a two-dimensional representation, much like Montessori's golden beads grounded children in the reality of numbers and values before they experienced calculating symbols.

## Matt Sees Shapes

Our son, Matt, grew up around markers and crayons and was often testing ground for new revelations that would later be confirmed in Young Rembrandts' classroom experiences. One day in my home office, I drew out a checkerboard lesson with Matt, who had just turned three. We drew five lines across the page horizontally, then five vertical lines, creating a checkerboard pattern. In a regular class setting, the children are directed to choose one crayon, trace around the inside of one of the

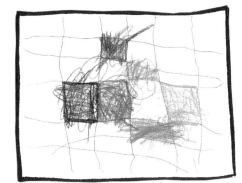

squares and then fill that square with color.

He had a hard time "seeing" the squares created by the pattern. So I asked him to choose a crayon. I outlined one of the squares and helped him stay on task until it was all colored in. He chose a second color, I outlined another square and he filled it with color. We repeated this process four or five times, and then it hit him. He suddenly "saw" the different shapes created by the intersecting lines and understood the squares. He exclaimed, "Aha! I get it. I put a new color in each of the boxes" and proceeded to color the squares independently.

Over the years, I had seen many children color in coloring books. It's very common for young kids to scribble color all over the page, oblivious to the individual shapes within the image. Eventually, most children make the perceptual leap and do see the small shapes within the larger image and apply color accordingly. But this experience with Matt allowed me to observe the exact moment he made that shift in perception. He went from seeing a page with random lines to seeing the individual segmentations his intersecting lines had created. This was an enormously significant transition in his visual perception skills and would benefit him in multiple ways. Understanding this transition helped me fine-tune my teaching method and intentionally create opportunities for this type of visual-spatial training in our pre-school and elementary classrooms.

## Learning to Draw

Once we finished "seeing" and had a basic understanding of the item we were going to draw, I passed out paper and pencils, and we started the drawing process. While looking at the drawing of the object, I carefully led the students through the step-by-step process of drawing it. With my own paper and pencil in hand, I drew and they drew. First, we placed the larger shapes that defined the object. I demonstrated how to make the shape; they watched, listened and then drew the shape themselves. We were careful about where to place those first shapes, the position on the page, and drew large enough to fill the page with our drawing. While instructing, I used reference points, like the sides or middle of the paper, once I defined them and was sure they had understood. Using reference points increased their awareness of size and space and the relationship between shapes. Once the basic shapes were placed, we added additional lines, shapes and details to complete our drawing. We all learned to draw the same object, yet each child's personality was evident in their drawing.

## Ashley & Frankenstein

A delicate little four-year-old named Ashley, dressed in her customary girly girl pink and purple, attended my drawing classes on Monday afternoons. Her brother and she had been in class for several months, with their younger brother waiting to start next year when he turned three. One October afternoon, we were learning to draw Frankenstein. Ashley was in class that day, but her older brother was absent. As I introduced the subject matter, we talked about this fictional character, carefully analyzing the shapes that made up his long face, large forehead, big nose and oversized ears. The students were especially interested in his oversized mouth, crooked teeth and multiple sets of stitches.

As the group talked and drew Frankenstein, Ashley had an extra air of delight about her. In fact, she was simply tickled about Frankenstein, giggling and smiling all throughout class. Finally, I asked what was making her so happy. She said, "I'm going to know how to draw Frankenstein and my big brother is not."

## Learning to Color

After learning to see and learning to draw, the class learned to color. Teaching kids how to color is often overlooked and undervalued. Learning to color is a very significant process and provides a fun, multisensory way to develop fine motor skills, extended time on task, organization and many other critical learning functions. A single drawing is composed of a multitude of smaller shapes, and coloring it is a complex process requiring multi-step sequencing. Children need to know where to begin, how to organize the activity and how to follow a logical order of progression. Instruction that includes a predictable, replicable method enables students to learn to order and sequence a multi-step process. Much like the Montessori classroom, critical learning skills can be developed while children are engaged in thoughtfully developed, fun activities. In our class, this complex, multifaceted learning took place while kids were relaxed, coloring.

As children develop fine motor skills, they also need to know how to use their pencils and markers. This will affect them in the art classroom, but more importantly, in every other part of their school day. Along with mastery of their pencil skills, I was delighted to teach my young students the kinds of techniques I learned at the design house. Each week, I demonstrated coloring techniques that were adjusted to their age and readiness level, understanding they would be adopted as each child was physically and mentally able. While we colored, we talked about color, about finishing small parts before larger areas and about how to fill very large areas with color. We were also careful to complete each space before we moved on to the next.

> " *A single drawing is composed of a multitude of smaller shapes, and coloring it is a complex process requiring multi-step sequencing.* "

## The Most Beautiful Headdress

Paige, a four-year-old Montessori student, had been in class week after week for several months. She listened well, followed directions and was openly enthusiastic. Yet her drawings didn't reflect the understanding she demonstrated in class. When the coloring portion of class came, whatever she had been able to draw was usually obliterated under a chaotic mess of crayon or marker. Each week, I touched base with Mom, sharing news from the classroom. Each week, Mom enjoyed whatever Paige completed and was pleased she had participated. Each week, my own doubt grew and I began to wonder if, in fact, I really could teach **any child** how to draw and color. And each week we pressed on, approaching every new lesson with expectation and enthusiasm.

One day, we drew an Indian headdress, a day forever etched in my mind and heart. Our class had been drawing together on Monday afternoons for nine weeks. On this particular Monday, the students gathered, took their usual places at the table, and we looked at a real headdress. We talked about the shape of the headband, the tall feathers standing upright and the designs and colors. As we began to draw out the lesson, I took special note of Paige. Her fine motor skills seemed more controlled, and it was reflected in her work. Her drawing was full of wonderful detail and really looked like an Indian headdress! As we began to color, we followed our usual coloring techniques, and again Paige moved through this part of the lesson, clearly demonstrating increased abilities.

While I was silently jumping up and down with delight, Paige proceeded as she did every week, faithfully drawing and coloring with all her heart. When she finished, we mounted her drawing, as we did every week. She smiled, as always, and headed back to her regular classroom. I was moved to great emotion, as I admired the **most beautiful** drawing of an Indian headdress. In just one week, there had been a profound transformation of Paige's abilities, and the proof was on the paper. When her mother came to view the week's drawing, it was with tears in my own eyes that I presented Paige's finished piece. Mom was pleased as always and an extra wide smile crossed her face.

> " *Every week that Paige had been in class listening, looking, drawing and coloring, she was processing every bit of the learning experience. But her physical body had to catch up with her mental processes.* "

The event signified a broader kind of understanding for me. Every week that Paige had been in class listening, looking, drawing and coloring, she was processing every bit of the learning experience. But her physical body had to catch up with her mental processes. When her fine motor skills increased, her hands could finally do what her mind could conceive. Everything she had been exposed to over those nine weeks came pouring out of her that day. Paige continued to operate at this new level, and each week her drawings reflected her increased abilities. Over the years, this experience has been repeated in many classrooms, with many other students, but Paige and her Indian Headdress will forever hold a special place in my heart.

6

## Art Talk

While coloring with my students, I was also intentional about developing language skills around art. This added to their vocabulary and gave them experience talking about their art and art they were viewing. They  learned the names of colors; "wild strawberry" and "granny smith apple" were favorites. They learned to talk about their art, but our conversations weren't about like or dislike, pretty or nice. We learned to explain the art we were doing and to describe the elements of art. We talked about shapes, lines, colors and patterns. We learned about perspective, vanishing points, horizon lines, cold and warm color palettes and more.

I was also intentional about taking the emotions and labels out of the art experience. This is where so many negatives can become attached to art and can limit the freedom to learn and explore. It's important to separate the art from the person doing it, especially when it comes to motivating and evaluating. We didn't make "pretty" pictures or do art for Mom — we did art because it was there to do. Students weren't good or bad because of their art — they were students doing art.

I was also mindful of using less language, and delivered my instruction in smaller bite-sized chunks. In special education, this is referred to as "chunking", but I have found it enormously successful with learners of all ages. Young children, visual-spatials and auditory-sequentials are often overwhelmed by too many words. This is the root of so much misunderstanding and misbehavior. So in art class, my language, influenced by my Montessori days, was simple, informative and direct. If there was something that wasn't done or understood, I explained it again and directed them back to the task at hand. No one was made to feel wrong.

The language in our class was age-appropriate, direct, encouraging and always positive. This process of simple, clear information, direction and redirection minimized behavior problems. They had a clear understanding of what was expected and a feeling of safety. If they didn't understand or wandered off track, they would be led gently and positively back into position. The how-to instruction and visual demonstration gave them the information they needed.

## Playing Art Class

Over the years, I have heard many stories about children playing art class. It seemed the language we used in art class was so unique — kids were using it at home. What seemed especially significant to the parents was the way their kids were using "art talk" with their friends.

My friend, Linda, shared an "art talk" story. One day, her four-year-old daughter, Beth, one of my pre-school students, had two friends over. During their afternoon together, they decided to play art class. The three girls gathered around the kitchen table with paper, pencils and crayons and became engrossed in activity. Mom was out of sight, but listening to their conversation. As the girls drew and colored, they talked "art talk."

Mom heard them saying:

"That orange and purple look really good together."

"You are being very careful in your coloring."

"My favorite color is magenta."

"Please pass the yellow orange."

"Be sure you cover all the white spots on the page."

"Remember to outline the shape before you color it in."

After repeatedly hearing these stories from parents, I became even more aware of the power of the language and its affect on our students. I was delighted to hear they were modeling the language, as they drew and encouraged each other.

## Pre-School & Elementary Success

Each week, as I worked with and observed my pre-school students, I learned more about skill sequencing, varied the level of challenge based on individual readiness and fine tuned my language and presentation skills. I learned as much as my students learned, and together we discovered the world of guided drawing instruction for pre-school students. My young students participated in drawing class with open hearts and minds, delighted to see what they could draw — often surprising themselves. Throughout our class experiences, the kids were very pleased with themselves. Their confidence grew, they felt empowered and parents reported an increase in drawing time at home. Parents also reported seeing increases in other skills like attention to detail, longer attention spans and improved fine motor skills. It seemed that what we were doing in drawing class was benefiting them in other areas.

> *...students weren't just learning to draw. They were developing critical learning skills such as attention to detail, increasing time on task, completing a cycle of activity, organizing, sequencing and working through a multi-step activity with ease.*

My work with pre-school students gave me additional insights for teaching elementary students. Pre-school and elementary students have similar developmental needs, so many of the presentation techniques and strategies I used in pre-school classes were incorporated into teaching elementary students. Their inclusion brought the entire educational experience to a heightened level. My pre-school and elementary students weren't just learning to draw; they were developing critical learning skills such as attention to detail, increasing time on task, completing a cycle of activity, organizing, sequencing and working through a multi-step activity with ease. Elementary students need to develop these same skills, so I became more intentional about verbal and visual vocabulary, added art terminology and extended our observation exercises to foster increased visual acuity, patterning and differentiation skills. The more I honed my teaching method, the more impactful the multi-tiered learning became.

## Taking It on the Road

After a couple of years teaching classes and developing curriculum, I decided to expand my class offerings. At that time, several of the national day care center chains had started to offer "extra" programs, such as dance, computers and science. These classes were held at their facility in the mornings, once a week, as a convenience to working parents. Parents paid extra for these classes and enjoyed the convenience of the daycare location. So off I went, knocking on doors asking to hold Bette's Art Classes at their facilities. The first few day care centers I approached didn't ask much about my teaching philosophy. They checked my references and looked to see if they had room to add another ancillary program. Once I established classes in one center, word spread, and I was welcomed at many other locations.

I also approached Montessori and other independently owned pre-schools. Several pre-schools, especially educationally-based programs, paid close attention to the quality of programs they allowed in their schools and carefully reviewed my teaching method before scheduling classes at their school. Once classes started, they observed me in the classroom and grew confident about the work I was doing with their students. Over time, my enrollment expanded to two hundred students a week at a variety of locations. I dropped my own kids off at school and taught several classes each morning, my original Montessori pre-school classes Monday afternoons and my elementary classes at home on Thursdays. Life was busy, intense and fun.

# Defining a Philosophy

As I began teaching to a larger customer base, I had more exposure to the early education community. It helped me clarify and further define my own teaching philosophy. While the majority of facilities I approached welcomed me, some were opposed to teaching children how to draw. At one particular pre-school, I met with the director and gave her a detailed explanation of my teaching philosophy. I showed her my curriculum, some student drawings and carefully described the positive, fun classroom experience. After the presentation, the director looked across the desk at me and said, *"What you are doing is wrong."*

She reached into her files and pulled out a copy of a poem. As she pushed it across the desk towards me she said, *"You're ruining children."* I quickly scanned the paper in front of me, fighting to hold back tears. I was completely taken aback. The poem talked about boundaries and control, implying that using them while doing art was death to a child's creativity. I mumbled some lame reply, took the poem and quietly exited the school.

Safely in my car, the flood of tears came. I loved children. I loved teaching children. I loved unlocking their potential and giving them tools to expand their abilities. I loved seeing the joy in their faces as they conquered new frontiers. The very thought that I was doing something that would cause any kind of damage pierced my heart. More tears came. Still sitting in my car, I reread the poem she gave me. At first glance, there seemed to be some validity to the author's position. But the more I read it, I realized the poem wasn't about art. It was about styles of teaching that control and suffocate, *regardless* of the subject matter. That's not what I was doing. Kids get training in all sorts of things. Education is about giving information and managing a classroom so learning can happen. But I was giving kids "how to" information in art. That was the objection. The director had mistaken giving this information as control and restrictions that would hinder their creativity. This can be a common misunderstanding.

My tears beginning to subside, I thought about what I was doing with my young students. I thought through the classroom process and the way my students learned multiple aspects of every subject we drew. Their vocabulary increased, their understanding grew and their artwork continued to surpass expectations. They were happy, learning, improving and creating — always hungry for more.

> " *Training doesn't limit personal expression.*
> *It's quite the opposite. It empowers.* "

I decided to disregard the director's well-intended comment and trust the children and the success I had experienced in our classrooms. This process of *guided instruction in art* left plenty of room for personal interpretation and creativity. Personal expression and technical skill are two separate entities. My instruction developed technical art skills, just like training on a musical instrument develops technical music skills. Training doesn't limit personal expression. It's quite the opposite. It *empowers*. Being technically proficient brings confidence. Skill and confidence undergird personal expression. Training develops the skill needed to express oneself. I had seen this time and time again in my classes. Giving information didn't limit or hinder my kids; it actually enabled them to do more.

## Before & After Drawings

Whenever a director agreed to offer my classes at their pre-school, I held demonstration classes for all of the three to five-year-olds. These demo classes allowed the staff to observe my teaching method and watch the children participate. To start class, I asked students to draw a person's face — any face — any way they wanted. They put their names on their drawings. Afterwards, they were thanked, complimented, and we set them aside to do another drawing. Before the next drawing, we spent time looking at a face, noticing the shapes, details and feature placement. Then I used my same method of guided instruction to teach kids how to draw a face full of all the details we had observed. Once we started drawing together, their faces filled the page, their eyes had circles inside circles, eyelashes and brows, hair became more defined and their personalities shone through brilliantly.

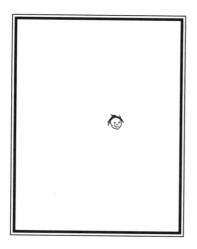

**Before Instruction:** *As directed, Olivia, a four-year-old student, drew a person's face. As sweet and endearing as it is, it is very small on the page and lacks detail. This is quite typical of pre-school drawings.*

**After Instruction:** *Once we spent time looking at a real person's face, and noticing the shape of a head, eyes, mouth and other features, we drew another face. Kids enjoy drawing what they have just observed and their drawings clearly reflect their heightened observation skills. Notice Olivia's large, oval shaped head that fills the page. Her detailed eyes, eyelashes, eyebrows and big smile with little square teeth complete her drawing.*

Every time I did these Before and After Classes, they yielded impressive results. The finished drawings were very effective indicators of how much children could learn in 30 minutes. The dramatic improvement in abilities often prompted parents to enroll their kids in weekly classes. In some cases, the school was so impressed that they hired me to teach weekly classes to all their pre-school students.

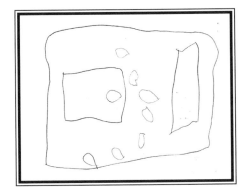

***Before Instruction:*** *Four-year-old Kyle had a basic understanding of the shapes used to draw a house, door and window, but was unable to complete his thoughts.*

***After Instruction:*** *With observation and instruction, Kyle's house is on the ground, has the door and window in place with a roof and chimney to complete it. Because he was able to better organize the elements of the house, he was now able to add many supporting details: grass, bushes, flowers and sunshine, to tell the rest of his story.*

## Resistance to Change

There were times, even with a successful demonstration of increased ability, that I encountered resistance to my teaching method. At one particular day care center, I had spent the day doing classes for sixty pre-school students, then proudly mounted all the drawings and shared them with the school staff. Everyone agreed the results were remarkable. Students took their drawings home with pride. Pleased with the day's activity, I packed up, anticipating strong enrollments and a great relationship with the school staff. But things didn't go as I had hoped.

The next day, I got a rather unusual phone call from the director. She was upset and said one of their students had come back to school asking too many questions. It turned out one of the five-year-old students had really enjoyed learning to draw the detailed face and went home and repeatedly drew new faces. Pleased with her understanding and newfound mastery, she came to school the next day asking how to add a hat to her face drawing. The staff teacher she asked wasn't able to answer her, and instead of seeking out information for a curious child, she saw a problem.

The staff talked it over and decided more teaching would risk more questions they didn't know how to answer. They told me, "Children should be content with the abilities they have and will figure out anything else on their own." The director decided not to offer drawing instruction to their students, so art class was canceled.

> **66** *...this misunderstanding that information stifles creativity is stopping us from teaching the visual arts in a more impactful way.* **99**

The opposition and challenges to my methodology caused me to further investigate existing art education philosophies. It helped me better define my philosophy and better articulate this new realm of possibility for children and art education. There are still many educators who believe demonstration and guided instruction in visual art will stifle individual creativity. They were educated to believe creativity is developed through creative experiences, and that information, guidelines and too much structure will limit what a child will create independently.

In most pre-school settings, children are provided wonderful tactile and sensory experiences using art materials, like easel and finger-paints, to explore and enjoy. At this young age, making an impact on their environment — making things happen

— is very important. Smearing bright red paint on paper satisfies this sensory need, as does cutting, rolling clay, stamping and ink. Craft projects with paper, scissors, paste and glue help develop fine motor skills and the ability to sequence and follow directions. In some cases, but not all, pencils, markers and crayons are on hand. Yet with all the materials they are given, there is little if any organized instruction.

In the elementary classroom, there is very little time devoted to teaching art. Budgets are strained, and the arts are not highly valued in our test-focused education system. What little time there is for art instruction has to cover a vast array of media experiences, art awareness lessons (viewing famous works of art) and some may even include lessons that would be considered craft projects. And while budget cuts and lack of funding are significantly limiting art instruction, this misunderstanding that *information stifles* creativity is stopping us from teaching the visual arts in a more impactful way.

When children are provided art instruction, skill training is limited to the use of actual physical tools like scissors, glue and paint. It doesn't include the "how to" of seeing and making visual symbols — drawing. This is a critical tool for our visual learners, but also a crucial component of learning to do art.

## Crisis of Confidence

Children grow weary of doing art without instruction. This leads to what art educators call the "crisis of confidence." Eventually, kids realize their stick figures don't look like the person they wanted to draw. They get bored and disheartened when their images no longer satisfy them, and no one tells them how to make their stick figures into figures with volume and form. By their own evaluation and comparison, they grow discouraged. Without knowing how to take their images and abilities to the next level, they decide they're not good at art.

Sadly, the majority of young children will stop doing art. They stop drawing. They stop making. They stop enjoying art class. They remove themselves from all the benefits that participating in the arts can provide. And worst of all, they blame themselves. They stopped doing art because they thought they weren't good at it, when in reality it's the instruction that wasn't good enough. Some of the "art kids" will keep drawing. They like it enough to press on and figure some things out on their own. They have some innate artistic ability to get them through, but even they crave instruction and information.

Mothers often brought their kids to my class at this critical transition time. Their child had no confidence in their abilities and stopped doing art. These parents didn't want to settle for limitations, especially at such an early age. They sought out ways to rebuild their child's confidence and ability. Once in my classroom, their child learned the "how to" of art. They learned how to **see**, how to **understand** shapes and symbols and how to **draw** shapes and symbols. They learned to add the patterns, details and personality that told their stories. Every week they learned to draw something new, and over time, they gained the fundamental skills and confidence to draw whatever they wanted to draw. They gained confidence and continued doing art because they were given the information they needed.

## Getting Past the Crisis

A concerned mother brought her son, Sean, to a Young Rembrandts class. Sean informed his kindergarten teacher that he "did not do art" because he "was not good at it." He told her that his friend, David, was the artist, not him. This wise mother didn't want this self-imposed label to limit her child, so she enrolled him in class.

On Sean's first day of class, the students were learning to draw a fish. He joined the class and worked alongside the other students, including his friend David, the "artist." One step at a time, they learned to draw a fish. First, they drew a large oval shape. Then they added a large tail, fins and one eye at the front of the oval shaped body. Students used wavy, straight and zig-zag lines to create patterns on their fish, adding seaweed and other details to complete their underwater scenes. During the coloring portion of class, they learned marker and coloring techniques. Sean easily kept pace with the other students. He learned as they learned and successfully completed his drawing.

As we stapled and mounted the finished work, Sean looked around beaming with pride. When his mother arrived, Sean greeted her with excitement and said; "Mom! Mom! Look! I am an artist!"

## No Crying in Pastel Class

Young Rembrandts is focused on teaching drawing, because like music, dance and creative writing, artists need to know the fundamentals of making images, while having opportunities to create and express themselves in other media. Drawing is to creativity what reading music is to playing the piano, practicing positions is to dance, or grammar is to writing. There have been times we taught other media and found students still needed the step-by-step "how to" of drawing the subject they are going to paint or ink. The competency gained while learning to draw provides children with increased confidence as they approach other art media. This is a story of some revelations that came while teaching pastel classes.

As my family art business grew, the fax machine was in the bedroom and laminator in the laundry room, we decided it was time to move out of our home office. We leased office space for our growing staff with an area for a good-sized classroom. During the school year, we conducted morning classes for Home School students and afternoon classes for pre-school and elementary students. In the summer, we offered a variety of themed drawing camps, such as Super Hero Drawing Camp, Cartoon Camp, Under the Sea Pastel Camp and Horse Drawing

Camp. These camps used our same "how to draw" teaching method, but were organized around a specific subject matter, with students meeting for longer classes several times in one week.

Any new curriculum we developed was first tested in our classroom location, enabling us to refine and improve our teaching materials before our instructors taught it at other locations. This was especially significant the first time we taught Horse Drawing Camp, where students were introduced to pastels. This particular class gave me enormous insight into the challenges children face when using unfamiliar media with difficult to draw subject matter.

It was mid-July, and our camp class was comprised of fourteen eight to twelve-year-old girls, all eager to draw horses. On the first two days of camp, students learned to draw the horse's head and upper body. They drew it over and over again from different angles, changing the markings, backgrounds and scene details. The girls used colored pencils to complete their drawings, focusing on color choices and coloring techniques. The class was doing well; students were enjoying themselves and feeling very confident. Day three's lesson would be our first full horse figure, completed in pastels.

We started class by looking over the planned drawing. It was a full figure of a horse, complete with those tricky shaped legs, the long, wide neck blending into the body and the overall proportion challenges that distinguish a horse. We talked about the basic shapes, distinguishing features, proportions and placement on the page. Next, we talked about pastels, being careful to thoroughly introduce this new and unfamiliar medium. We practiced drawing and coloring with pastels on small papers to build our experience and comfort level.

As the instructor, I led the girls through the drawing portion of the lesson using a light colored pastel to draw our horse. When drawing our first full-figured horse, there were some new and significant things to learn. Step-by-step, I demonstrated and they drew. First the head, then body and leg guidelines, and gradually we saw

 our horses take shape on our special pastel paper. Yet even with careful step-by-step instruction, something besides drawing was happening. Rather than the growing confidence I typically sensed from my students, there was increasing frustration and discouragement. The drawings were not meeting their expectations.

Drawing a horse's body was a challenging subject, but drawing in pastel, a new and unfamiliar medium, added additional difficulty I hadn't anticipated. The pastel was too clumsy to use, not a match for the delicate lines of the horse's body. The first two days of class they had drawn in pencil and could easily erase what they wanted to. Erasing with pastels was more complex and less satisfying — leaving smudges and smears all over their paper.

I encouraged, helped and redirected throughout the drawing portion of class, and we made progress. Eventually, we got to the coloring portion of class, and as each student followed my instruction and began to fill their page with color, there was excitement. But the further along we got in the coloring process, the more their frustration and disappointment grew. One by one the tears began to flow, until everyone was miserable. What had challenged them in the pastel drawing process was made worse in the coloring. The tears weren't about using pastels; they were about the students' unmet need of what they desired their beloved horse to be and what appeared on their paper. The more the drawings came to life in full color, the worse it got. Their drawings were still not meeting their expectations and they felt little hope of making them better.

Now, I have met with some frustration in class — it's infrequent — but it happens. I have easily helped the student gain the understanding needed, but this was the first time my whole class was in tears. Quite surprised by the situation, I spoke some encouraging words and rushed to the Young Rembrandts office across the hall for help. I quickly explained, and several well-trained instructors rushed back into the classroom with me to help quell the tears. As a team, we worked with every young girl to get their horse drawing to be as realistic as they desired. For some of the younger students, we added long grass in the field to cover up what they didn't like about those difficult to draw horse legs. Some kids added fences to hide bodies or added other scene details to camouflage their disappointments.

While we rescued, we talked about how artists find solutions. We made sure they understood the difficulty was in the subject and medium, and not in them. We talked about what it takes to keep working on something until we reach the desired goal. In the end, everyone was smiling again, proud of their finished piece. And everyone had gained some confidence and strength from going through the process.

This challenging and emotional experience brought me several key revelations. It was absolutely heartbreaking to conduct a class that brought children to a place of such frustration and disappointment in their work. It was a poor choice on my part to expect children to master a complex drawing while using an unfamiliar and relatively complex medium. It was unfair to expect them to master two very different challenges simultaneously. They should have been on solid ground with the subject matter before they learned how to use pastels to add color and form. And I needed to be sure the level of difficulty was well-matched to the media and age group.

The value of testing our curriculum was validated, and we made the needed adjustments. We still draw horse heads and full-body figures, but save the pastels for a horse composition they can all complete successfully. I am happy to say that after teaching thousands of drawing and pastel classes over the years, there has never been another wave of crying in art class.

## Expanding with a Mission

After several years of teaching, I saw how giving students information changed them. I saw how it impacted their art and overall learning abilities, but there was more to it. These kids stayed involved in the arts. They saw themselves as more able, creative and confident in other areas. Parents reported increased attention to detail, time spent on a task and better performance at school. Knowing I was making a difference made me hungry to reach more kids, so I decided to expand Bette's Art Classes. I hired a few teachers and trained them to use my teaching method while I continued to develop curriculum. Much of what I was doing in the classroom had become intuitive (as it was based on my education and experiences), so I needed to be sure my teaching method was replicable. Thankfully it was, and as the number of instructors increased, my classes and enrollments grew. Broadening the application and variety of instructors using my method continued to refine and sharpen the predictability of the success we could have with every student.

Eventually Bette's Art Classes evolved into Young Rembrandts classes. "Young" — because my students were young. "Rembrandts" — because I wanted to name our classes after a revered master artist. Rembrandt van Rijn (1606-1669) was known for his incredible technical drawing and painting skills, as well as his contribution as an artist.

After a few years, my husband Bill left corporate sales and helped me expand my fledgling business. We continued to add staff and accounts, expanding into additional markets. We started classes at park districts and recreational facilities, offering pre-school, elementary drawing and cartoon classes and camps. Our classes were very popular, and these facilities were pleased to work with a professional education company that had a depth of curriculum, staff and experience.

Eventually we approached local elementary schools and offered our classes after school. The program was offered to the whole school, and those children that wanted the additional art training stayed after school one day a week to draw and learn with us. Our program became a staple, with families enrolling their children semester after semester. Elementary schools saw us as an educational partner and a strong supplement to their existing art programs, and the expanded art offerings increased awareness of the arts and reinforced its value in their community. Art kids and non-art kids enjoyed the social aspect of attending art class, just as kids enjoy the social aspect of being on a sports team.

Over the years, Young Rembrandts has grown into a national and international business, reaching tens of thousands of children a week. We are honored and excited to work with so many students. Our instructors are a passionate breed, enthusiastic to share the secrets of art and delighted, too, by their student's successes. When I hear instructors' stories from the Young Rembrandts classroom, view student art work and hear what parents are observing in their children, I remain passionate and resolute in our mission to equip and empower children through the development of foundational art and visual communication skills.

# The Future for All

As a visual-spatial person, I have felt wrong, unequal, and not good enough. There have been times when I didn't understand or value my ways of thinking. Even when doing well, I felt like an imposter, trying to fit in and be like everyone else. But I finally know who I am, where my strengths lie and where my weaknesses can trip me up. As I have become more aware of my learning and thinking style, I appreciate my intelligence and abilities and have been able to learn what I need to be more effective. I am still wary of tests, and have accepted that it takes effort to memorize dates or details, and to prove in order to persuade. But I also now know there are times it's worth the effort.

I also have a deep affection for children. I love to teach, help, encourage and love those who are understood as well as misunderstood. I have been eternally blessed to spend my life working with and for children, their whole lives ahead of them and the answer to our future. Children, created in perfection, can encounter serious challenges in this perilous world and we — parents and educators — are their safe haven, their lifeline. They see themselves through our eyes. They define themselves by our opinion, our assessment. When they're met with eyes of recognition, acceptance and safety, they can relax and get on with the business of becoming. But to live easily in the position of full acceptance, understanding and compassion, we have to be willing to really see them, not as who we think they should be, but as who they really are. There are a multitude of attributes for what some would call "deficits." It's a choice in the eyes of the beholder. It's not about them fitting into our systems, our expectations, but about us being open to see and do whatever needs to be done, even if it means changing ours paradigms, our fixed ideas and ourselves. It's imperative we give heart, soul and the fullness of ourselves for all children to thrive. It's our responsibility to help all children develop the gifts, abilities, and thinking and learning styles that innately suit them.

With increased awareness and adjustments to current assessment and educational methods, we can break the cycle of underachievement, low self-esteem, shame and confusion. Understanding will enable us to parent and teach in ways that allow our children to excel, feel confident in themselves and treasure the uniqueness of who they have been created to be.

As we raise this visual generation, confident and able to use the unique strengths of both their left and right hemispheres, we will prepare them for a future that embraces linear and non-linear, text and context, logic and intuition. The profound impact of these innovative and disciplined minds will be reflected in our schools, communities, businesses and the global marketplace.

# REFERENCES

[1] Hoffer, Eric, *Reflections on the Human Condition* (HarperCollins, 1973), 22.

[2] McGilchrist, Iain, *The Master and His Emissary* (Yale University Press, 2010), 27.

[3] Pink, Daniel H., *A Whole New Mind: Moving from the Information Age to the Conceptual Age* (Penguin Group, 2005), 3.

[4] Drucker, Peter F., *Managing in a Time of Great Change* (Harvard Business Press, 2009), 189.

[5] Pink, Daniel H., *A Whole New Mind: Moving from the Information Age to the Conceptual Age* (Penguin Group, 2005), 14.

[6] Silverman, L. K., Ph.D., "Identifying visual-spatial and auditory-sequential learners: A validation study," N. Colangelo & S. G. Assouline (Eds.), Talent development V: Proceedings from the 2000 Henry B. and Jocelyn Wallace National Research Symposium on Talent Development (Gifted Psychology Press, 2000), 5.

[7] Eisner, Elliot W., *The Arts and the Creation of Mind* (Yale University Press, 2002), 196.

[8] Grandin, Temple, *Thinking in Pictures: My Life with Autism* (Random House. 1995), 3-4.

[9] Silverman, L. K., Ph.D., *Upside-Down Brilliance: The Visual-Spatial Learner* (DeLeon Publishing, 2002).

[10] http://www.whitehouse.gov/the-press-office/president-obama-expands-educate-innovate-campaign-excellence-science-technology-eng, accessed October 2011.

[11] West, Thomas G., *In the Mind's Eye* (Prometheus Books Publishing, 1997), 244.

[12] "Global Literacy Challenge: A Profile of Youth and Adult Literacy at the Mid-Point of the United Nations Literacy Decade 2003-2012," United Nations Educational Scientific and Cultural Organization (UNESCO, 2008).

[13] Comer, Michael W., Frankie Troutman and Jo Anne Vasquez, *Developing Visual Literacy in Science, K-8* (National Science Teachers Association Press, 2010) 28-29.

[14] "Multimodal Learning Through Media: What the Research Says," Metiri Group, Commissioned by Cisco, Fadel, Charles and Cheryl Lemke. 2008.

[15] Freire, P., *Education for Critical Consciousness* (Seabury Press), 1973.

[16] Falihi, Anahit and Linda Wason-Ellam, "Critical Visuality: On the Development of Critical Visual Literacy for Learners' Empowerment," *The International Journal of Learning*, Volume 16, Number 3, 2009. 413. http://www.learning-journal.com.

[17] Duffelmeyer, Barb Blakely, & Ellertson, Anthony, "Critical visual literacy: Multimodal communication across the curriculum," [Electronic version]. Across the disciplines, 2. 2005.

[18] Falihi, Anahit and Linda Wason-Ellam, "Critical Visuality: On the Development of Critical Visual Literacy for Learners' Empowerment," *The International Journal of Learning*, Volume 16, Number 3, 2009. 412. http://www.learning-journal.com.

[19] "vocabulary." *Merriam-Webster.com*. http://www.merriam-webster.com. Accessed November 2011.

[20] Elley, W.B., "Vocabulary Acquisition from Listening to Stories", *Reading Research Quarterly* (1989), 174-187.

[21] Silverman, L. K., Ph.D., *Upside-Down Brilliance: The Visual-Spatial Learner* (DeLeon Publishing, 2002), 70 (Appendix C).

[22] Sir Ken Robinson presentation, http://www.ted.com/talks/ken_robinson_says_schools_kill_creativity.html, Filmed February 2006. Accessed September 2011.

[23] Silverman, L. K., Ph.D., "Identifying visual-spatial and auditory-sequential learners: A validation study," N. Colangelo & S. G. Assouline (Eds.), Talent development V: Proceedings from the 2000 Henry B. and Jocelyn Wallace National Research Symposium on Talent Development (Gifted Psychology Press, 2000), 5.

[24] Freed, Jeffrey, M.A.T. and Laurie Parsons, *Right-Brained Children in a Left-Brained World: Unlocking the Potential of Your ADD Child* (Fireside, 1997), 24.

[25] David, Ronald D., *The Gift of Dyslexia: Why Some of the Smartest People Can't Read... and How They Can Learn* (Penguin Group Publishing, 1994), 38, 66.

[26] West, Thomas G., *In the Mind's Eye* (Prometheus Books Publishing, 1997).

[27] Dixon, John Philo, Ph.D., *The Spatial Child* (Thomas Books, 1983), 23.

[28] Sword, Lesley K., "I think in pictures, you teach in words: the gifted visual-spatial learner" http://www.giftedchildren.org.nz/national/article4.php. Accessed July 2010.

[29] Silverman, L. K., Ph.D., *Upside-Down Brilliance: The Visual-Spatial Learner* (DeLeon Publishing, 2002), 11.

[30] Haas, Steven C., "Algebra for Gifted Visual-Spatial Learners", *Gifted Education Communicator* (Spring 2003), 30-31; 34; 42-43.

[31] Sword, Lesley K., "I think in pictures, you teach in words: the gifted visual-spatial learner" http://www.giftedchildren.org.nz/national/article4.php. Accessed July 2010.

[32] "Tossing the Script: The End of the Line for Cursive?" Brian Braiker, www.abcnews.com, 2011.

[33] Berninger, Virginia and Robert D. Abbott, "Relationship of Word- and Sentence-Level Working Memory to Reading and Writing in Second, Fourth and Sixth Grade," *Language, Speech, and Hearing Services in Schools* (Volume 41, 2010), 179-193.

[34] James, Karin Harman, "Sensori-motor Experience Leads to Changes in Visual Processing in the Developing Brain," Dept of Psychological and Brain Sciences, Indiana University, (Blackwell Publishing, 2009).

[35] Freed, Jeffrey with Anne Kloth & Julie Billett, "Teaching the Gifted Visual Spatial Learner," http://www.openspacecomm.com, 2006, 6.

[36] Freed, Jeffrey, M.A.T. and Laurie Parsons, *Right-Brained Children in a Left-Brained World: Unlocking the Potential of Your ADD Child* (Fireside, 1997), 137.

[37] Edwards, Betty, *The New Drawing on the Right Side of the Brain* (Penguin Putnam Publishing, 1999), 253-254.

[38] Grow, Gerald, "The Writing Problems of Visual Thinkers," School of Journalism, Media & Graphic Arts, Florida A&M University, 1994. http://www.longleaf.net/ggrow.

[39] Tulving, E., "Episodic and semantic memory," In E. Tulving & W. Donaldson (Eds.), *Organization of memory* (Academic Press, 1972), 385-386.

[40] Grow, Gerald, "The Writing Problems of Visual Thinkers," School of Journalism, Media & Graphic Arts, Florida A&M University, 1994. http://www.longleaf.net/ggrow.

[41] Nicholas, Robert, Ph.D., Ronnie Kauder, Kathy Krepcio, and Daniel Baker, Ph.D., "Ready and Able: Addressing Labor Market Needs and Building Productive Careers for People with Disabilities Through Collaborative Approaches," (National Technical Assistance and Research Center to Promote Leadership for Increasing Employment and Economic Independence of Adults with Disabilities, 2011).

[42] "creativity." *Merriam-Webster.com*. http://www.merriam-webster.com. Accessed November 2011.

[43] Wolf, Gary, "Steve Jobs: The Next Insanely Great Thing," *The Wired* Interview, 1996.

[44] "innovation." *Merriam-Webster.com*. http://www.merriam-webster.com. Accessed November 2011.

[45] Sir Ken Robinson presentation, http://www.ted.com/talks/ken_robinson_says_schools_kill_creativity.html, Filmed February 2006. Accessed September 2011.

[46] Silverman, L. K., Ph.D., *Upside-Down Brilliance: The Visual-Spatial Learner* (DeLeon Publishing, 2002), 349.

[47] Doschka, Roland, *Pablo Picasso: Metamorphosis of the Human Form: graphic works, 1895-1972* (Prestel, 2000).

[48] Associate Dean of Animation, Sheridan Institute of Technology. 9/26/2011

[49] Montessori, Maria, *The Absorbent Mind 1949* (Kessinger Publishing, 2004), 8.

[50] Wesson, Kenneth A., "Early Brain Development and Learning: Part Two, The Learning Brain", http://www.sciencemaster.com.

[51] Butterworth, Brian, *What Counts: How Every Brain is Hardwired for Math* (The Free Press, 1999).

[52] Diamond, Marian and Janet Hopson, *Magic Trees of the Mind: How to Nurture Your Child's Intelligence, Creativity, and Healthy Emotions* (Dutton, 1998), 159.

[53] Wiesel, Torsten N., and David H. Hubel "Single-cell responses in striate cortex of kittens deprived of vision in one eye," *Journal of Neurophysiology* (1963), Harvard University, 1002-1017.

[54] Gardner, Howard, *Frames of Mind: The Theory of Multiple Intelligences* (Basic Book, Third Edition, 2011).

[55] Julia Ormond, playing Temple Grandin's mother, Eustacia Cutler, in the HBO film *Temple Grandin*.

[56] Grandin, Temple, *Thinking in Pictures: My Life with Autism* (Random House, 1995), 3, 26, 28.

[57] Ibid, 26.

[58] Kluth, Paula with John Shouse, *The Autism Checklist: A Practical Reference for Parents and Teachers* (Jossey-Bass Publishing, 2009), 112.

[59] Edwards, Betty, *The New Drawing on the Right Side of the Brain* (Penguin Putnam Publishing, 1999), 4.

# INDEX

## ABOUT THE AUTHOR

Bette Fetter, founder and CEO of Young Rembrandts, Inc., began her career as a professional artist with a Bachelor of Fine Arts degree from Northern Illinois University. Through her education, participation in various forms of the arts and experience with Montessori education, Bette gained first-hand understanding of the value of the arts on developing young minds.

Her passion for the arts and early childhood education led Bette to develop Young Rembrandts, a unique teaching methodology focused on developing foundational art and drawing skills in young children. Bette franchised her business, and what began 24 years ago with eight kids at her kitchen table now reaches tens of thousands of children nationally and internationally.

While writing *Being Visual*, Bette received her MBA from Roosevelt University in Chicago, Illinois. Bette is the President of Brilliant Arts, a non-profit organization whose mission is to provide and support arts programs for children that aid in the development of neural and cognitive learning skills.

Overall, Bette's mission is to reach children and adults alike in order to "raise generations that value the power, the passion and the significance of art." Bette has four adult children and lives with her husband in Illinois. For more information on Young Rembrandts, visit www.youngrembrandts.com.